THE LITTLE MONSTERS TAROT GUIDEBOOK

OLIVIA EPHRAIM PEPPER & PEONY COIN ARCHER

the little monsters tarot guidebook

WELCOME

thank you for choosing little monsters tarot. we are very pleased to have you with us and along with this new deck, you are also holding both of our intentions that these cards will serve you well.

there are many ways to welcome a new deck into your life, but i prefer this one.

sit with the cards in your lap. open a window. take a deep breath and close your eyes. what do you smell? what do you hear? how do you feel today? keep breathing. shuffle the cards a few times with your eyes still closed. listen to the sounds they make as they move in your hands. you're getting to know each other! this is a relationship that could last a very long time. whenever you are ready, i like to ask, simply: "what is the first lesson you will help me learn?" and then pull a single card.

open your eyes. what do you see? what did you get? what does it mean to you? where will you go from here?

bon voyage, and many blessings.

much could be written on this subject, and much has been, but the best method for reading tarot can be boiled down to a few very simple directives.

get quiet within yourself.
take your time.
trust your intuition.

as you read through this book, don't just take my word for it - the cards have many deeply layered meanings and each one contains an entire world of symbolism. additional research can be done as to the cards' traditional and historical meanings (there are many wonderful books and resources available online), but what is most important is what they mean to you personally. and i mean this, from the bottom of my heart. you are the expert on your world, and i trust you. hopefully the cards will only help you to trust yourself more.

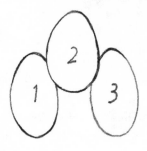

NEST

this spread is especially useful for understanding what resources you have at your disposal to address a specific, singular issue. if you have questions about the overall nature of something: a relationship, a conflict, a job opportunity or another upcoming challenge, try this layout.

three cards, each with equal merit, nested alongside one another. their overlap is not coincidental. these are three cards that have equal bearing on the situation at hand, and their interpretation is meant to be read in combination. these cards represent what you bring to this specific issue, and thus, what you may be able to expect to experience as you move forward.

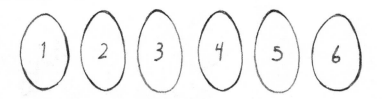

BUTTERFLY'S EGGS

six cards, laid out in a row, which can more clearly divine the nature of a particular path you are considering taking.

1 - the beginning, the origin
2 - your motivation
3 - the current state of this path
4 - a block or challenge to be surmounted
5 - the lesson contained within this path
6 - a possible final outcome

this spread is suitable for charting the course of just about anything, but is especially useful when checking in on something that has a timeline of around six months to a year.

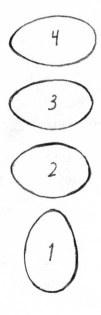

SEEDS

four cards, for when you are trying to make a decision. the first card, at the base, represents an objective. the following three, that which bury the seed, illuminate the questions or challenges that may arise from putting focus on this particular seed.

(note: because of the alignment of the top three cards, the "upright" cards are those on their left side, with the name of the card on the right; "reversed" are those on their right side, with the name of the card on the left.)

here are the 22 big lessons of life, the movers and shakers of the tarot. they show the glorious path of human experience from start to finish, and they help us to understand where we are at on that path. each of these 22 trumps are worlds unto themselves, and each of them could take a whole lifetime to understand. what we hope is that we have channeled each lesson into an image whose symbolism can be understood, whose meaning can be grasped.

these are the big lessons in life, rising above the material complaints of the world. these are the cards that show us who we truly are.

note: while the minor arcana in the little monsters tarot includes divinatory descriptions for reversals, the major arcana is a little different. the energy stays mostly the same, but when it is reversed it shows that it is blocked by something: by denial, disavowal, or a lack of material resources. for example, the star reversed is the same as the star upright, it is just unseen through a haze. the chariot reversed is your cab waiting just around the corner. strength reversed is a side of yourself that exists, even if not publicly. the hermit reversed is finding solitude even in a crowd, zoning out, tuning out. and so on, and so forth.

THE FOOL

keywords: trust, newness, a bright change
gemstones: aventurine, herkimer diamond
herbs: white rose, any sprouting seed or sapling

the fool's number is zero (0), like an egg containing all of the potential for new life, or a seed just waiting to grow. if the fool tumbles into your reading today, you could well be holding a whole new life in your hands.

usually the fool turns up for us when we are engaged in dauntingly new life experience. perhaps it feels scary to be so alone in doing something you have never done before. perhaps it feels like everything is changing, and there's nothing you can do to stop it. perhaps you don't understand why any of this is happening in your life.

that's ok! most of the time people don't understand anything, really. we might think we do but we are usually wrong, because things are always changing so fast it is hard to keep up with understanding anything.

the fool takes us to the place of trusting strength that exists in not-knowing, in having some faith in the big weird mystery of the universe, in following the flicker of life where'er it may lead. if everything has changed (or if it has to soon), then so be it. strive to live openly alongside that change.

fools can be seen as sacred if we want to allow room in our hearts for this: they are those who can be seen embracing the strange, the unexplained, the unknown, and dancing with it. look at all this chaos and overwhelm in your own life and try the same thing: try dancing with it.

that number zero is a big beautiful circle: what goes around comes around, all things have their end (and beginning!) and life is an endless miraculous cycle.

the fool is asking you to trust that this is the right place and the right time, even if it feels like you're stepping into the void.

THE MAGICIAN

keywords: action, ability, personal power
gemstones: bloodstone, cinnabar
herbs: vervain, astragalus, dill, star anise

well, well.

it looks like you have everything you need to do whatever your soul most truly desires. what luck! and what responsibility!

the magician's number is 1, also stylized as I - and that's no coincidence. what we have here is a moment in time -a magical, perfect moment- when everything is about you, the individual. it is about being accountable to yourself as much as it is about being ambitious on your own behalf, but this is certainly about your power in the world.

if you've been waiting for your time to shine, you are probably already shining. if you wish to seize the day, open your hands and see the sunlight on your palms - you've probably already done it!

the magician corresponds with times in our lives when we awaken to our own power as a conduit for the vibrant aether that creates our world. you, too, can create your own reality, and there is no need to delay - whatever you want, you can have!

but be careful! it is imperative that you listen carefully and dutifully to your own soul's message. all of this power you have now could easily get spun out of control and you could end up with something you thought you wanted that, when it takes root in your life, doesn't look anything like what you actually wanted. be mindful and heed your private inner voice, the one that knows all.

sometimes the magician suggests that you are hungry for ritual, arcane knowledge, for a sense of doing your own magic.

go ahead! make it up if you have no examples that you like of this sort of thing. that's all anyone else has ever done anyway.

THE HIGH PRIESTESS

keywords: intuition, patience, mystery
gemstones: pearl, moonstone, blue kyanite
herbs: acacia, pomegranate, sandalwood, lilies

maybe you've heard before that we are all made of stardust,
that all of the iron in our blood came from stars that exploded
long, long ago.

maybe you've also heard that atoms move about somewhat
unimpeded by our ideas about the laws of the material world,
shifting around and changing in ways invisible to us.

the high priestess is content to disintegrate in every moment, to be never not falling apart into dust and chaos, to be reborn in the next moment from one speck, one seed, one atom that leads the charge. this falling apart sounds dramatic, but it is a private process for the high priestess. it is a neutral process. it is quiet and almost looks dormant, just like atoms shifting unbeknownst to us. this disintegration is a phoenix rebirth that happens so quietly and in such a deep part of yourself that no one else can see it and you can't explain it. it is holding yourself suspended between poles, like those pillars that the high priestess dissolves between: you are between good and bad, time and timelessness, black and white.

the high priestess is, in fact, the gray area, and also represents the gray matter: the brain, that glorious tool of knowledge and analysis that we are all bestowed.

everything we have ever learned, however banal, is to serve us in this life. we are each of us vast encyclopedias of knowledge, carefully curated for our particular life, and we have every answer that we might need carefully catalogued in our subconscious.

the high priestess is urging you to get quiet, get still, and be a good librarian of the self. you know the answers already - they are in there somewhere.

THE EMPRESS

keywords: fertility, connection with nature, abundance
gemstones: emerald, rose quartz, moss agate
herbs: basil, myrrh, apples, wheat

all potential is contained within this divine spirit. here is the
archetype that is often assigned to the feminine: that which is
receptive, nurturing, fertile and eternally abundant. all things
are possible when the empress comes into play. she brings with
her such fullness, ripeness, and ability. i often see clients
unconsciously sigh with relief when she appears. she brings
unconditional love with her, the bounty of the universe. she

promises that you were brought into this world for a special purpose, and that she will nurture you in that purpose.

being ruled by venus, the empress represents all things beautiful and nurturing to the eye. she also suggests the concept of pregnancy and fertility - which of course can be physical or can represent something else: a project, a plan, or a story coming to fruition. surrounding her are emblems of the harvest: wheat adorns her like a crown, she rests in prolific flowers. her very touch brings forth life.

if the empress comes to you, she bears a message of deep contentment and joy. she is ready to receive you, to allow you to rest your weary head in her lap and believe in your own starry potential. you are a seed that the empress will water and sing to, will watch grow. know that you are adored by the universe, and that the universe has equipped you with the ability to give back in exchange for the remarkable blessing of life.

but remember: you cannot pull up clean water from an empty well. if you have given too much, or been asked for more than you have, remember that although your heart bursts with love, you cannot bow to these requests or you will make yourself barren.

THE EMPEROR

keywords: discipline, focus, discernment
gemstones: carnelian, obsidian
herbs: ginger, tobacco, rosemary

the emperor represents stability, security, decision-making, personal power - all the things traditionally associated with the "masculine" or "yang" energy. he is ruled by the planet mars, historically linked to war and conflict - and this association is important, but the truth about the emperor is that he is a peacemaker. he has the ability to settle conflicts swiftly and gracefully. he has power because he has respect. he has authority because he has studied. he is committed to values of fairness and equity.

peony has drawn a forward-facing emperor, and what a formidable monster he is! traditionally, the emperor is shown in profile, as if to emphasize that he uses one half of his brain more than the other, separating emotion from logic. however, what we see here represents a new take on the traditional aspects of this card: a transforming energy that allows for compassionate discernment. no coincidence, either, that he holds a wand instead of the traditional sword (or arrow, as the case would be here). instead of utilizing the weapon of the mind, our emperor uses the power of his spirit to make conscious choices in the world.

when the emperor arrives, we can know that we have close at hand a right use of power, an ability to lead, to govern - either ourselves or our projects. however, the emperor is careful not to waste his energy on meaningless power struggles, as you should be also.

THE HIEROPHANT

keywords: striving, mystical education, awakening
gemstones: topaz, smoky quartz, ruby
herbs: gardenia, passionflower, saffron

the hierophant is my nominee for the most misunderstood, and
possibly misrepresented, card in the entire tarot. to many
people, the traditional imagery brings up feelings of religious
suppression or some kind of squicky masonic shady business.
and there is no question that organized religion is responsible
for some of the greatest ills that we face in the world, and that
this card has historically borne symbolism related to religiosity.

regardless, the longing for spiritual wholeness and union with the divine is present in everyone, even the atheists among us. whether you find your communion in a church or a chatroom, a forest or a dancehall, we all need the kind of link to the higher world that the hierophant describes and lays out before us.

in essence, this card represents the yearning for and curiosity about what lies beyond our realm of knowledge and awareness. the hierophant holds this dynamic down, and is therefore also called "the magus of the eternal gods." see, the hierophant knows what's up in the universe. the hierophant knows the names of newborn stars and the songs they sing to one another, but also knows the life cycle and arc of the smallest snail. the hierophant murmurs praise to a blooming daffodil and laments an ancient fallen city. the hierophant compresses time and distance and meaning into graceful little loops and letters, wisdom that is more easily accessed and dispensed.

of course, being a priest ain't easy, and the hierophant carries some heavy burdens in their quest to bring this information to the world. the key here (and i use key deliberately, as it is a potent traditional symbol associated with the hierophant) is that there is no true release from the suffering of mortal existence but death, and that as long as we are alive we will be separated from the divine - but that this separation, and the urge to close it, is an essential component to who we are. with increased openness and attention paid to the meaning of things, whether your own meaning or part of a larger system, you can find islands of relief as you navigate your particular story.

THE LOVERS

keywords: intimacy, empowerment, choice
gemstones: watermelon tourmaline, emerald
herbs: ginseng, patchouli

everyone is always so happy to see the lovers turn up, and i always have to bite my tongue to keep from telling them that they shouldn't necessarily be so thrilled.

only because love is terrifying - because of course it is. what else could it be?

the lovers represents the powerful moments in our lives when we are called upon to learn things that we cannot possibly learn on our own, to surrender to the lessons that come from uniting ourselves with someone whose spirit has called to us across the void, since time immemorial. sometimes this isn't even representing the traditional love relationship, but merely a deep and profound connection relating to art, family, friendship, or business. we all have connections that weave their way into the tapestries of our lives, and the lovers is a surefire sign that one of these sacred connections is playing out in a big way in our lives.

there is also a profound choice represented here, the moment of truth, when we decide to go toward something or to turn away. there is always, always some measure of self-sacrifice involved with a true surrender to what is offered by the lovers. in ideal marriage, for example, there is a seeming paradox between the selflessness involved in giving yourself entirely to another person and saying you would do anything for their wellbeing, but also a deep selfishness inherent in containing or imposing your own will upon that person's destiny, in aligning and linking your fates.

while the most traditional way for the lovers to turn up is when someone is actively making that life-changing decision about whether to align themselves to a spouse or partner, it can appear in many different places in our lives, but it is always asking: how much are you willing to give in exchange for divine union?

THE CHARIOT

keywords: action, individuality, movement, change
gemstones: pearl, citrine
herbs: st. john's wort, daisy, lotus

associated with the cardinal water sign of cancer, the chariot
also rules over the period of time in our lives when we become
cognizant of our own individuality and thus, our own power. i
remember being absolutely enamored of this card when i was
eight and nine years old - perfect timing, as i was coming into
my own skill, ability, and empowerment with the world, and
understanding how i could control my own destiny. you might

be feeling similarly if the chariot makes its way into your reading.

the chariot appears in times where we have to take individual action to change our lives, but also when we must take care to exercise caution and discretion. cancer, the crab, is armored and can conceal its soft parts from attack or intrusion. in peony's rendition of the chariot, the monster rides atop a mutable shape concealed by a starred tapestry, very traditional symbolism within the card, representing all the myriad possibilities that each of our fates contain. i love this choice because it speaks to what i see as the chariot's truest meaning: exerting loving, cooperative control over the mysteries of the emotions.

the pursuit of self-knowledge is inherent here. with each choice we make, each step we take, the idea is to know ourselves better along the way. the chariot definitely calls for change, for movement, for action, but in a way that emphasizes building trust with the unconscious at every step. there can be some struggle here -looking at ourselves honestly is not always easy!- but the end result will be deeply, deeply worth it.

STRENGTH

keywords: power, faith, self-love
gemstones: green tourmaline, diamond
herbs: cedar, sage

what i like to tell everyone when we are exploring the strength
card is that both monsters are incontrovertibly part of the self:
the innocent, trusting, wide-eyed monster and the ferocious,
ravenous, bestial monster. and while some interpret strength as
having "power over" or transcending outside circumstances, i
almost always see it as having "power within" and undergoing
the alchemical processes of self-transformation.

what we might see as a power struggle between the two monsters represented in the strength card is actually a unity, harmony, synthesis - or it can be, if it is done right. think of what jung called "the shadow self." we all have it. we all have greed, deceit, viciousness, and selfishness in us. we all have beasties. we also have naivete, trust, openness and vulnerability. either of these, in imbalance, can cause us great harm, but when they are united as one front we can trust the entire world, because we can trust ourselves.

often strength arrives when a querent is really struggling with an aspect of themselves, something they wish they could just get rid of and run away from. strength is an invitation to tame the self through trust. what would be possible if you trusted yourself more?

THE HERMIT

keywords: solitude, isolation, introspection
gemstones: sapphire, merlinite
herbs: angelica, tea

our hermit holds a glowing sphere in place of the traditional lantern, like a little illuminated planet, a whole world aglow with eerie light. within its depths, who knows what the hermit has learned to see?

around the hermit's feet we see dandelions gone to seed, ready to disperse their possibilities into the rest of the world at the first gust of wind. this is a gorgeous metaphor for one of the most valuable meanings of the hermit card: that this is one who has gone out into the wilderness of the soul to learn, and can illuminate the path for those who are to follow.

it may be that you've experienced a depression, a period of grief or loneliness, a great loss - often folks who see the hermit a lot have a bit of an outsider complex going on, or have retreated from the world as a way of avoiding additional tragedy on top of what they have already gone through. the hermit began their journey in the material world, after all, and suffered there, and retreated into their own personal wilderness because of this suffering.

because of that aspect, we have to be careful not to linger too long in our own isolation. virgo, with whom this card is associated, is at its worst when it makes itself a martyr, and so is the hermit. all that wisdom is useless if you don't share it, you know?

THE WHEEL OF FORTUNE

keywords: transition, fate, destiny
gemstones: turquoise, red jasper
herbs: clover, spearmint

around and around we go, forever and ever, on the rollercoaster of life. sometimes we're up, sometimes we're down, and sometimes it is hard to know where we are at all. the wheel of fortune is a confusing card simply because in some ways it represents divine confusion. why do good things happen to bad people? how do villains succeed? who doles out all of these lots in life, anyway?

the wheel of fortune often arrives in my clients' readings when they cannot believe their luck - either for better or worse. how could something have gone so wrong, or so right? basically the wheel of fortune reminds us that we are not in control. our experience with the chariot, strength, and the hermit may have made us feel that we got this shit on lock, but the truth is we don't even know the half of it.

once the hermit makes the decision to go out and help the world with the glorious information they have gathered from the depths of solitude, new mysteries are presented and embodied by the wheel of fortune. round and round we go, and why nobody really knows.

but one thing is certain, and that is that there is no stopping the ride. you just gotta go with it and see what it holds for you. so hang on, and smile for your picture at the top.

JUSTICE

keywords: equilibrium, understanding, logic
gemstones: amazonite, garnet
herbs: jasmine, acacia

while justice can represent fairness, a decision made in the querent's favor, or a settled court case, i most frequently see justice come up to represent injustice on a global scale. now, i know that sounds confusing, but let me explain. justice is a lesson in karmic responsibility. every person who is spiritually inclined has at some point wrangled with the questions stirred up by the wheel of fortune: what kind of benevolent universe allows rape and genocide and starvation and war crimes? how could justice possibly exist as long as there is so much suffering?

in short, justice is our call to align ourselves with what is right and true in the universe, to create patterns of balance that ripple out into the universe beyond our small lives. it is not so much a question of why these atrocities exist in our world, but in how you respond to them. this is on a major collective scale and also on a more intricate and personal level: so you see someone in your neighborhood who needs help, who is hungry, who is afraid - what will you do to help? so you have experienced abuse or violence - what will you do to care for yourself, to keep yourself safe?

true justice does not trouble itself in analyzing why oppression exists, but in what actions it can take to exterminate it.

THE HANGED MAN

keywords: transformation, self-sacrifice, enlightenment
gemstones: black tourmaline, sugilite
herbs: seaweed, yew

our hanged man wears a hood, perhaps hinting at the card that is to come: at death. and indeed, this is a kind of execution, albeit one the hanged man has signed up for willingly. this card's story is associated with the myth of odin, who volunteered to be suspended between worlds for nine nights in exchange for sacred knowledge, sacred information.

i see this card come up for people very frequently when they are putting themselves through hell, with the expectation that something good will come from the effort. remember when justice asked you to create balance and right the scales? the hanged man recognizes the sacrifice necessary to do just that and steps up, volunteers, submits, surrenders. to be quite blunt, i see this card a lot when people have hit rock bottom or a brick wall and have realized how desperately they need to help themselves, whether with mental/emotional issues, gender confirmation, substance abuse, or a very challenging revelation about a relationship or family dynamic.

such glorious transformation is possible here. it is going to suck, make no mistake. you are going to wonder if it was worth it, all this pain, all this suspension, all this agonizing patience. but you will emerge completely changed, and the truth is, that's what you want most desperately.

DEATH

keywords: transition, release, acceptance
gemstones: jet, diamond, mica
herbs: marigold, roses, anemone

everyone is so scared of the death card all the time, but it is such a sweet little blessing, i promise you. it is not at all about bodily, physical death - although it does sometimes come up in readings where the querent has experienced a loss, that is just because it represents how profoundly loss changes us.

the death card is basically a rest stop in the desert, with a picnic table underneath a magnificent cottonwood tree, where you can stop all the hubbub of everything and just be for a minute, where your mind can be empty and your spirit attuned to its deepest truth. it is a reminder that we are all the same, all perfectly made, that everyone has struggles and triumphs and that nobody gets out of here alive, anyway.

deep, profound compassion, represented by the rose on death's banner, is the true meaning of our lives. remember the empress, with her unconditional love? that love is a gold thread woven through every aspect of our lives, even lives of almost complete suffering. death gathers everyone up, with a profound gentleness, everyone from killers to kings, and recycles all of our atoms into other things. death will always accept you, no matter what condition you are in.

and being able to tap into the energy of death while we are still living represents the ability to totally change...after the agony of the hanged man, we are now something totally new! revel in the newness, the transformation. let go of all the old illusions, and step through the veil to the next phase, to the next life.

TEMPERANCE

keywords: balance, creativity, alchemy, androgyny
gemstones: iolite, amethyst, rainbow moonstone
herbs: iris, valerian

they call temperance "daughter of the reconcilers." and yes, temperance blends everything, all elements of the self, and transforms lead into gold.

the suffering explored in the cards preceding this one now becomes the glimmering stuff of personal triumph, personal influence, flowing out into the world like a river of light. a perfect analogy for temperance is an artist who has suffered immensely and transmutes their suffering into a compassionate and compelling work that has the potential to assist others in their suffering while at the same time alleviating the suffering of the artist. onward and upward goes the transformative energy of temperance.

temperance is certainly associated with profound acts of creativity, of bringing forth, as well as of reconciliation and forgiveness, but it is especially associated with a kind of serene determination. we say that metal is "tempered" when it is repeatedly struck to make it stronger. we say that emotions are "tempered" when they are handled carefully and with restraint, with balance. of course, temperance also has to do with tempo, or time.

a teacher of mine once told me a story about the origin of the phrase "this too shall pass." long ago, my teacher said, an emperor asks his philosophers and counsel to bring forth a simple, short phrase that would make him happy when he was sad, and sad when he was happy. the phrase that came forth? this too shall pass.

temperance understands this, and the querent soon will, too.

THE DEVIL

keywords: materialism, physicality, stagnation
gemstones: rhodolite, dravite
herbs: mugwort, bergamot

ok so the devil gets a real bad rap, but the message the devil brings is so, so, so necessary, especially in our current culture.

when temperance asked us to remember that "this too shall pass," the devil offers us a glimpse of what would happen if they didn't. what would happen if nothing changed, if we were stuck with things for eternity? without movement, without transformation, greed and control and misuse of power and commitment to excess and the grotesqueries of attachment to the physical world would have ample time to set in. the devil is a representation of someone who is rejecting change, someone who wants to hold on, who wants to control. this can be about lifestyle, or a relationship, or an aspect of the self. it can get really ugly, of course, with drugs and alcohol and sexual excess and self-abuse or abuse of others, but it is often stuck in our lives in subtle, unseen ways. after all, they say that the devil's greatest trick was convincing humanity that he didn't exist, yes?

so when the devil comes up in a reading, it is time to take a real close look at your life, at what is actually important to you and how your actions are matching with your objectives. if you look upon yourself with the silvery moderation taught by temperance, goals in the material realm will naturally fall away. money, beauty, reputation, power...under the light of loving self-observation, these become way less important than peace, meaning, connection, truth.

above all, be careful not to get stuck in patterns right now. extricate yourself from stories that repeat themselves. change things up. take breaks from the familiar and risks that you have never taken. question yourself.

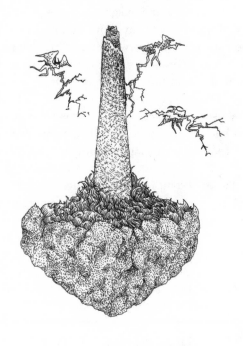

THE TOWER

keywords: collapse, destruction, disillusionment
gemstones: aquamarine, moldavite
herbs: garlic, morning glory

uh-oh. it is all coming apart, and there is nothing you can do. in fact, all you can do now is fall, and hope to be spared. the tower represents the chaos of job loss, divorce, a health scare or death in the family, a complete rearrangement of the self. frequently this collapse has to do with something that you were too confident in, maybe even arrogant about, something you believed would last forever (the devil, that seducer, with

permanence on his breath, made that promise, and we all know
how deals with the devil go).

the tower card is associated with the biblical tower of babel,
which was meant to rise to the heavens so that its builders
could confront and destroy god. the tower is also associated
with the hebrew word for mouth, and it has all sorts of
associations with language and communication - especially
with that idea that although we can trick ourselves with ornate
words or clever thought patterns, we never really truly know
what anyone else is thinking and, in fact, run the risk of creating
our own narrative to satisfy our desires - which will inevitably
crash down eventually.

so this is all really scary and overwhelming - what can you do?
the truth is, all you can do is let this come down around you,
and learn your lesson. it is ok, lessons are part of being alive. if
you welcome this change, it can be for the better.

THE STAR

keywords: hope, illumination, surrender
gemstones: amethyst, phantom quartzes
herbs: sweet hyssop, bluebell, vervain

in the aftermath of the tower's fall, all goes quiet and still, and
then in comes the hope i promised, that scrap of joy at the
bottom of pandora's box, that little emblem of courage blinking
in the inky dark - the ability to rebuild from what is left in the
tower's wake. although things will never be the same, they will
be ok - likely even better than they were before.

in the little monsters tarot, the planetary cards wear their
meanings in their vestments. they are almost like deities
arriving to earth, full of rich symbolic messages, and when i
look at peony's drawing of the star i can almost see its carefully
contained light leaking out from under its robes. the star
sometimes turns up when people are feeling super bummed,
super hopeless, like nothing will ever get better. i often see it
emerge for people who are suicidal - carrying that feeling that
they have lost everything and there is nothing left for them.

but look at the star, with a compass sewn over its heart. it
knows the way. you know the way. fix your eyes on a guiding
star and follow it. you will recover, you will taste the light
again.

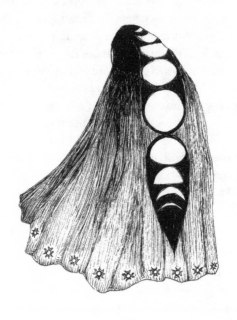

THE MOON

keywords: mystery, loss, questions
gemstones: apophyllite, tourmaline-included quartzes
herbs: eucalyptus, poppy

a-wandering we go, out into the unseeable mystery of it all.

the moon shows up for us in times when we are shaken to the core, unable to avoid dramatic and often unpredictable shifts in consciousness. yet while it can feel, to the querent, as if everything is slipping away or swelling uncontrollably, like an oceanic tide, we can see, if we just get far enough back, that

these cycles have a sense to them, a waxing and waning, a
fullness and an emptiness and then a fullness again.

the word "lunatic" has its origin with the moon, and indeed,
this card rules over all manner of mental complaints and hard
aspects, but also over deeper, almost shamanic knowledge.
you'll note that the robes of the monster representing the moon
have a ceremonial air, a beautiful profundity in their
symbolism. that's because this creature understands, deeply, the
path to true self-knowledge. it goes between the towers, it
winds out of sight, it takes you to places you have never dared
to tread before.

be ready, when the moon rises in your reading, to do some
serious exploration in the realms of the unknown, the unseen,
the untouched. you are embarking on a journey of the soul that
may get darker before it gets brighter again, but that's all part of
the story, and you owe yourself the complete version, not just
the cliffs notes.

wrap yourself up in your wandering cloak and head out. there
are secrets waiting for you to discover, pearls of wisdom to
collect in the great unknown.

THE SUN

keywords: joy, optimism, vitality
gemstones: sunstone, golden apatite
herbs: chamomile, sunflower

there's a feeling, and i know you know it: that feeling is lying blissful in the sun, half-asleep and drifting, warm and full of light, slipping happily between worlds. maybe you last had it in childhood, maybe you have only ever heard mention of it, maybe (if you're lucky) you just had that feeling recently. whatever the case, that feeling is contained here, wrapped up in golden paper like a luminous gift, reflecting light upon the monster's happy upturned face, symbolized by the blazing image resting golden on its back which illuminates its spine.

the sun is a symbol of the return to rightness. not righteousness, just rightness. the knowledge that everything in the world is in order. even in its chaos, its brutality, its loneliness, there is still this vast sense of golden trust that can exist. no coincidence that in alchemical practices, the sun is connected with the human heart: that battery that fills us with electric power, with the will to do good works, with strength and with life.

when the sun comes up in our readings, a whole new world is dawning around us. the message here is that we can always, always choose happiness. nelson mandela once said: "live your life as though nobody is watching, and express yourself as if everyone is listening." that is the message of the sun: humility, innocence, trust and joy, but also confidence, belief in oneself, virtue and pride. you are good enough, you are good enough, and the rays of the sun sing this song as they fall upon you.

JUDGEMENT

keywords: truth, awareness, spiritual awakening
gemstones: amazonite, charoite, jade
herbs: grapevine, violet, agrimony

here is another card, like the hierophant, that is frequently
rejected or misunderstood because of biblical or religious
connotations. but the true meaning of judgement is nothing to
reject or be afraid of - it means you no harm, even if it is going
to rearrange your whole worldview. in fact, judgement day as it
is represented in the tarot is nothing like what evangelicals
would have you believe. yes, it is evocative of the mystical

moment when the archangel blows into their trumpet and the dead rise up and the truth is made visible, but that truth is that we are all aspects of divine law. there is no punishment, no hell - only a sense of profound purification. the world must be cleansed before it can begin again.

in the little monsters tarot, our judgement carefully and serenely balances between two staffs, two wands, two souls, two epochs. the monster bears on its shoulders, almost like a burden, the even-armed cross which represents the unification between the ethereal and the material. all over the world, and for thousands of years, the even-armed cross has symbolized the unification of all elements, the cosmic reunion. here, at the end of all things, every lesson we have yet learned in the course of the tarot's teachings is synthesized into the biggest, most awe-inspiring truth we have ever known. there is a reason that the part that tells the end of the world in the bible is called "the book of revelation."

judgement comes up when all is revealed, all is suddenly clear, the path is open, the lessons embodied. even if it doesn't feel like that, that's what's happening. maybe it feels like things are slipping away or being lost, but whatever is going on is just part of the process of being purified, of ascending. often when a querent finds the judgement card presiding, it is a sign that very soon nothing will be the same. all manner of beautiful things are unfolding - this is really one of the most psychedelic cards in the tarot, the glimpse of the world's bigness, its perfection, its complexity. trust yourself to receive, and open your eyes to the divine.

THE WORLD

keywords: completion, wholeness, divinity
gemstones: sapphire, agate
herbs: bay laurel, vines

you did it! you made it! celebration is in order, and relief, and awe, and splendor.

the world holds before its heart a sphere, a disk, an orb, the congealed essence of everything that has come before, all the potential in the universe. it condenses and pulls inward, drawing in energy for the next big bang, so the whole damn thing can begin again with the fool's bright tumble into the aether.

the world is called "the great one of the night of time." whoa! "the great one of the night of time." how about that? you are close to experiencing whatever it is that we name god. you can see it all spread out before you, and you should take some time to look at it, to appreciate its marvelous splendor. what an accomplishment! even if the world turns up in your reading in a relatively mellow position, relating to a single completed project or a seemingly simple relationship breakthrough, it is not to be overlooked! rather, it is an indication that are breaking through all manner of karmic blocks, creating whole new worlds with your actions, and with your thoughts. there is so much glory here! you are truly experiencing what it means to be one with the universe - which, of course, comes from the latin universus, which means "combined into one."

everything you have experienced in your life thus far has played an essential part in delivering you to this precise moment, and this moment is a crucial part of the world's story. we may just be the universe experiencing itself, dead stars writing their memoirs upon flesh and blood, but whatever moment you are in now is a moment that the universe simply could not do without.

there are 56 cards here, almost all of which correspond with our modern pack of playing cards - except the four knights - they got taken out because they done got uppity.

i call this first group "the matter arcana," rather than "the minor arcana," as a lot of decks do, because these are not minor affairs, just because they rule over the simpler aspects of our lives. they do govern affairs of the material world, for the most part: the first 56 cards of the tarot rule over all of the actions we can take in life, all of the choices that guide us in creating the ornate architecture of our individual lives.

THE WANDS

the suit of wands, analogous with clubs in traditional playing cards, represents the transitional time between spring and summer, when the world is heating up and plants are growing in profusion. thus they rule over things that are moving quickly, things that are in development or things that are new (friendships, relationships, career paths, ideas). they also represent one's creative, social and religious life, and are closely associated with a querent's spirit or sense of self, to ego or personality. traditional associations include the element of fire, youth or childhood, the cardinal direction south, and the fire signs of the zodiac: aries, leo and sagittarius. in addition to this, the wands tend to represent the circulatory system, sanguine temperament, and athletics, so they may indicate that a person benefits from or could benefit from calisthenic activity - a way of "burning off" excessive temper.

when a reading is predominantly wands, it usually means there are a lot of creative ideas or new things in a person's life - they often come up in abundance when someone is beginning a new romantic relationship, when they have recently made a significant move, or when they are pursuing a change in career. sometimes (especially with abundant reversals) a lot of wands in a reading can represent what might be called "excessive heat," and may indicate tempers running high or a lot of blocked energy, or an excessively self-centered point of view. especially if no major arcana cards turn up for deeper guidance, this can represent a restless, tumultuous time, when one might feel like they are agitated and unable to focus. often this will be a time to "fight fire with fire" and engage the body in physically demanding activities, or to unleash blocked creative energy with artistic projects that are not results-based, like dancing, sketching/contour drawing or free writing.

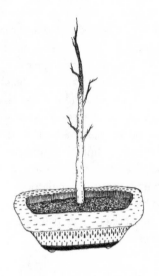

ACE OF WANDS

some of my nicknames for this card: the big bang; the spark; the genesis of life.

this is where the universe starts. sure, it is the fool who strolls endlessly around the edges of the zero, tracing infinity and representing the end / the beginning / the end and so on, but truly the ace of wands is something from nothing, a sudden bloom of life, fire brought to the earth people.

this card represents brand new ideas - lightbulb moments, breakthroughs, sudden realizations. It is a card of great potential...but if the spark is to grow into a flame, it needs attention and sacrifice.

in almost every mythological system all over the world, there is the story of a group of earth creatures going up into sky to retrieve fire and bring it down. it takes a lot of effort and experimentation, and usually there are some minor burns involved.

in this card, peony has illustrated a grounded fire: a wand planted in a pot, the metaphor being that this seed should be planted and nurtured in order to grow, that this bright jolt of inspiration must be transferred into material-world plans if its energy is to be utilized to achieve true personal change. (this is not to say that daydreaming and whimsy don't have their places in life: surely they do. but if the profound and potent energy of the ace of wands is to grow roots, it needs proper care.)

ace of wands could be the beginning of something great, something significant. or it could flicker and fade. the choice is yours.

ACE OF WANDS, REVERSED

a reversed ace of wands may indicate that you are having trouble deciding what you want. there might be a kind of snapping, electric energy about you that is without grounding or stability. you may feel like your nerves are shot, or that there are too many possibilities, too many choices. the key here is to settle this erratic energy. time alone may be indicated while you make up your mind. try looking at the other cards in the spread for additional guidance.

TWO OF WANDS

the twos represent partnerships and bonds, as well as decisions
- here, the two of wands represents a partnership within the
self: that of the lower self and the higher one, a spiritual
compact between oneself and one's internal muse or deity.

echoing the energy of the magician (just as the ace of wands
echoes the energy of the fool), the two of wands suggests that
the querent has everything they need at their disposal, but that
what is needed most of all is boldness, ingenuity and
willingness to take a risk - to get out of one's own way.

there is a promise here of investments paying off, of daring being rewarded, of the right path being naturally and easefully chosen when the decision comes from a place of deep trust in the self. do not be afraid to experiment, explore, or expand your horizons.

often associated with moving somewhere far away, making a daring business decision, undertaking a significant project, or taking a personal risk which involves showing a new aspect of the self.

power is a very important component of the two of wands: it is like a connected circuit suddenly bursting with usable electricity - funny that the two wands are a bit like two prongs attached to an electrical cord. what will you plug in? what will you empower?

TWO OF WANDS, REVERSED

two of wands reversed can indicate that someone is rushing headlong into unsafe territory without proper planning, caution or care, or that they are disconnected from the higher self. the feeling of youthful immortality runs high. risky decisions with money, personal power, or relationships are all possible. connecting with the higher self is paramount to success.

THREE OF WANDS

originally, the three of wands was about success in trade - in many ways this classical meaning still holds true. the three of wands is all about watching your ship come in: you've been working at something for awhile, have developed a good reputation (indicated by the garland of flowers draped over the figure who has all these wands to choose from), and you are ready to receive your due praise and continue your ascent.

it's all happening, says the three of wands. now is the time to look for even more opportunities, to level up. you're capable of even greater things now that you've made accomplishments and triumphed in certain areas of life. look for where you feel you have succeeded recently: in education, travel, business, career, creativity, spirituality, in relationships - and then invite yourself to look for ways to climb even higher. the energy is there.

THREE OF WANDS, REVERSED

Three of Wands reversed suggests wasted efforts, frustration, and delays or obstacles caused by others - issues beyond your control, or circumstances that feel like failure or a setback.

be careful not to expend too much personal energy when three of wands appears in a reversed position: there is a warning that too much investment in an untenable project or relationship could lead to burnout.

FOUR OF WANDS

a card of celebration, completion, family and the promise of
continued joy. i sometimes nickname this card "an Invitation to
a wedding," because it has to do with the process of actively
planning for one's own happiness, because it is a kind of r.s.v.p.
to your own joyous future.

often it represents a joyous occasion that will arrive in the
future: a birth, a graduation ceremony, a wedding, a reunion.

the seedlings have been planted and are being adored, being
cared for. there is an allusion in our card to the jewish festival of

sukkot, when bundles of plant matter are lifted into the air in praise of god. the four of wands is like this too: symbolizing a feeling of gratitude for what one has in life - giving thanks for good friendships, relationships, creativity, and enriching spiritual life. gratitude is the key to continued joy, and the four of wands is a reminder to give thanks for any and all abundance in your life.

relationships with family (whether chosen or biological) are important here as well, as is the understanding that all of our successes are due to the contributions and presence of others. as important as individuality and self are, no one is an island, and we do not create in a vacuum. we are interdependent. showing gratitude for your connections may be a good thing to focus on at this time.

FOUR OF WANDS, REVERSED

if four of wands appears in a reversed position it can be a sign that familial relationships are muddy or disharmonious. it may also indicate that the querent has forgotten to give gratitude for the bright things in life, and has fixated on the shadow or the pain. gentle redirection back to praising what is good can help.

if conflicts with friends or family members are an issue, try believing in a positive outcome rather than focusing on a worst case scenario.

FIVE OF WANDS

for years, i have nicknamed this card the card of false conflicts. take a look at the five figures in the card and perhaps you can see why. each is armed with their own staff, which they could use to fight, to playfully spar, to build a wall, to plant in the ground and see if they will still grow…there is competition between the figures, with each vying to express their own unique position.

but there is an invitation within this card to see things in a different way, to learn that what the querent may take for a conflict is actually something that can pass quickly or be solved through agreement, altered through positive thinking and a sunny perspective. the five of wands often comes up when discussing large-scale social justice issues, times when a lot of angry or frightened voices are competing to claim the title of most viable opinion, most emotional appeal - essentially a yelling match. on a personal level, the five of wands often reveals itself when the querent is going through an intense period of indecision or internal conflict: either about a large scale socio-political issue or something more personal like whether or not to leave a relationship.

in any of these cases, there are a lot of competing voices, all trying to overpower one another, and the best option may be cooperation, understanding, mutual empowerment. consider non-engagement, a period of stillness and reflection, self-examination.

FIVE OF WANDS, REVERSED

five of wands reversed is about not giving a damn. there may be a lot of conflict going on around the querent, but they just can't bring themselves to care. depending on the circumstances of the querent's life, this can be a good thing or a challenge. if not giving a damn comes about because of burnout, exhaustion, emotional fatigue, or hopelessness, it may be a suggestion to reinvigorate, to renew, to relight the spark within the heart.

but if it is a choice to ignore senseless conflict, to rise above, then five of wands reversed can be a benediction and a reward.

SIX OF WANDS

historically, this card indicates victory or completion, which comes with the ability to overcome obstacles and triumph over unfortunate circumstances. traditionally, the card shows a person, a standard-bearer, riding a horse (often white), through a cheering crowd, to indicate that victory has been visited upon the querent.

of course, in real life, victory is complicated. our six of wands suggests a challenge, a tipping point, a careful balance - all of which is very much an aspect of having a sense of victory.

challenges are real and are not to be overlooked. to achieve triumph, one has to be careful and cautious in the achieving.

now might be a time when you can express the victories you've achieved - but only with a sense of maturity, sophistication, and guardedness. the trials and travails you've experienced deserve a place at the table. your victory would not be complete without them. the sixes are cards that speak to knowing the self first and extending from a place of that self-knowledge, and here we see a figure who knows what they have accomplished but also recognizes the cost at which those accomplishments came.

go ahead and be bold, be brave, be bright - but do not be foolhardy.

SIX OF WANDS, REVERSED

six of wands reversed indicates that the querent has experienced a fall from grace. rumors, gossip or badmouthing may be running amok. unrequested criticism may have arisen, and often from an uninformed source. six of wands reversed suggests that plans may have backfired, social situations may have imploded, and the querent's reputation may be at stake.

now is a good time to pull back, channel energy inward, and see what kinds of internal reconciliations need to be made. please yourself before pleasing others.

SEVEN OF WANDS

this card is similar to five of wands in that it illuminates feelings of competition, strife and challenge; but here we see the implications of these struggles being about the self and not about the group. seven of wands is about the personal struggle to stay "on top," to maintain authority, to find a way not to lose face, to continue one's good work. this card may arise when there are professional challenges afoot, or when a querent is seeking information about a career change or opportunities within higher education. it is a card which comes up when one feels the need to prove oneself, usually in a larger context but sometimes with regard to familial relationships, intimate relationships, or creative accomplishments.

you can expect to be challenged when the seven of wands shows itself, but this challenge need not be a painful struggle - the querent can meet the oncoming challenge with courage, vitality, and experience. most of this struggle is internal: in traditional representations we see a person fighting off opponents who quite literally have the "lower hand" in that they are lunging upward with their attacking wands. in peony's rendition, our character balances carefully on one extended wand, emerging from an assemblage of other staffs - this image strikes at the true heart of this card, which is that the querent has everything they need to succeed but they must sink into themselves to do it.

think martial arts, and of the beautiful, listless, "in-between" space that the mind goes to during a sparring match: the perfect, illuminated moment when a fighter relies only on what they know of themselves and what they have been taught in order to succeed. all of the tools are before you. stop thinking so much and balance.

SEVEN OF WANDS, REVERSED

no two ways about it, the querent is overwhelmed. there may be a feeling of being under constant scrutiny, or always feeling like a failure. these feelings are real and deep, though they may not be as profound in the minds of others.

seven of wands reversed is a sure sign that the querent has said yes to too many things and is dog-paddling against the rising tide of responsibility. objective reasoning can help here. the same neutrality that helps win the battle when the card is upright can be employed here, to help see what is truly of use, what is truly necessary. cut out the excess.

EIGHT OF WANDS

in comes a great flight of energy! as sudden as a newly kindled
fire, crackling all around and lighting things up. this is a card
that flutters into readings when things are really taking off -
there is a sense that the blocked or challenged energies of the
seven of wands have cleared and rearranged themselves,
allowing for quickened vitality. a perfect analog for this
transition between cards appears (for the astrologically
inclined) when mercury goes direct after a period of retrograde.
reflection complete, life moves along at an enlivened pace. in
divinatory meaning this can mean a number of things, often
very dependent on surrounding cards: it could be that a creative

or business endeavor is taking flight after much preparation; it can also reflect things in a social situation suddenly coming to light or coming to a head. the many-winged birds surrounding the fruitful wands in peony's rendering of this theme suggest that there is much thought-activity present, that in the midst of our greatest creative breakthroughs we are suddenly flooded with new ideas; in the flurry of social or spiritual activity we may abruptly be granted new perspectives. allow space in your life for this giddy bright swirl. now just might be the time to fly.

EIGHT OF WANDS, REVERSED

ooof, here's the very image of mercury retrograde. communication and thought is confused, plans are delayed, mystifying obstacles crop up. there may be an abrupt shift in energy as things become increasingly convoluted. misunderstandings can be rampant when eight of wands reversed is in play. be cautious with your words, your deeds. try not to overcommit to a flight of fancy, nor speak out of turn. remember the gift of giving yourself time to think something through before making a decision.

NINE OF WANDS

we are so close now - almost there - just one more thing to overcome! nine of wands takes all of the creative, vibrant, passionate and lively energy in the eight cards preceding this one and translates it into the scene before us in which a wearied but still defiant figure, staff in hand, is prepared to defend the structure behind them. i have sometimes called this card "guarding the city gates" because there is a great sense of protectiveness about it - there is something dear and precious to the querent that must be defended, upheld, defied - a project, a partnership, a practice. traditionally, this card has also been called "the lord of great strength" because it shows how much we have learned and conditioned ourselves throughout the suit of wands, if we have been paying attention to the messages and lessons offered by preceding cards. in most renditions, the figure in this card is depicted as injured, as if nursing wounds from prior battles (think of the five, the seven), and is often shown to be exhausted or depleted. the meaning of the nine of wands, however, is almost always about having the strength to go on, to continue a project or see a dream through even in the face of difficulty, and to that end, peony has depicted this monster as one who may be confronted with an unexpected final setback, but is undeniably strong enough to complete this last push toward success. be attentive and mindful when it comes to what it is you are protecting, and know that you have the tools you need to accomplish your goal.

NINE OF WANDS, REVERSED

beware of paranoia and limited thinking at this time! in peony's version of this card, the figure wears an eye patch, suggesting that a painful event or experience may be creating temporary challenges to clear vision. often when we are hurt we become overly suspicious or reactionary, but wasting energy in unnecessary conflict can deplete our resources and take us further from the things we truly love. do your best to embody peace.

TEN OF WANDS

here we see a figure carrying with them a heavy burden. the creature is strong and upright, lifting its chin to the sky. In some versions of the ten of wands, the individual who bears this bundle of wands (ten of wands is called "the lord of oppression") walks with their head down-turned, their back to the viewer, their face invisible to the observer. our monster lifts its head to see forward, to triumph, and to look to the future. carrying many burdens and laboring under oppression is certainly hard work (and sometimes thankless), but the ten of wands tells us that all of our struggles are soon to manifest into fruitfulness. i often tell clients when they get this card that the wands depicted herein could go to any use: to incite a conflict or arm a group, to build a fence or a structure, to use as firewood or fuel, to be decorated and used within a celebration or ritual - and it's true! the ten wands borne by this figure, however onerous they might be to lug around, represent our ability to choose our perspective within a burdensome context. we are, in the end, the arbiters of our own feelings, and the ten of wands suggests that we choose carefully: what do you want to focus on? what is truly important? a cycle is wrapping up; what do you want your finished project to convey? you may have found yourself feeling overburdened or overstimulated. delegate tasks and responsibilities if possible, and see your course through to the end. reward awaits if your attitude can remain positive.

TEN OF WANDS, REVERSED

the time has come to take accountability for your own happiness and simplify. if there is a project you know in your heart that you need to give up, a job or relationship that you need to leave, ten of wands reversed is reminding you to act. it may be as simple as decluttering your home or work space, but the ten of wands reversed is a strong indicator that you have too much influencing you at this time, and that it is sapping your energy. there is not ever an easy or ideal time to lay down your burdens, but procrastinating can no longer be of aid.

CHILD OF WANDS

the child of wands never fails to bring an eager, curious, and slightly naive or experimental energy to any reading - in the hermetic tarot traditions, this card has been called "the princess of the shining flame," and its bright, fiery flickering illuminates all of the cards around it and infuses them with vivacity and excitement.

if the card illustrates an aspect of the querent's personality, it will likely touch upon the querent's innocence, curiosity, and ability to trust; if the child of wands is serving to represent an individual in the querent's life, it will be someone who seems young, naive, trusting, and immature, but also bold, artistic and unselfconscious, buoyant and adventure-ready. in some ways, the child of wands has a similar personality to the fool, bringing along that sense of blank-slate-ness, creative unrest and a feeling that one's circumstances are changing quickly. the child of wands has an irrepressible bright spark that can kindle just about anything, and often represents a new relationship or sudden inspiration coming from an unexpected source. If it is not honored, however, this spark can extinguish itself and cause depression, burnout, or ennui.

if the child of wands meanders into your reading, now would be a good time to follow your instincts and make bold and unconventional choices. there may be a bright new idea coming to you - something big and unexpected. honor your restlessness, your curiosity, but be careful! spontaneity is indicated, but not impulsiveness. try relating to the areas of your life ruled by the wands (creativity, social life, spiritual practice) with the attitude of a child. experiment and play, and see where it takes you.

CHILD OF WANDS, REVERSED

the child of wands reversed can be a bit of a troublemaker, as there is scattered, unfocused energy going everywhere. a lack of ability to finish projects, procrastination, diversion, distraction and on top of it all, a hot temper. when the child of wands comes up it is a reminder to cool down and try to limit overstimulation. if you can, take a day or two away from media of all kinds, external influences, technology and social situations, as all of these are providing kindling for an unnecessary fire. if the child of wands reversed represents a person within the querent's life, it is a person who is trying to proverbially "cut you down," someone who displays immaturity, competitiveness and a shallow approach. again, temporary withdrawal in order to gain perspective is necessary.

KNIGHT OF WANDS

look here at this fearless one! the knight of wands is the very embodiment of courage, ambition, and drive. where the child of wands represents a new idea coming in (like a match to tinder), the knight of wands represents the recently kindled fire, roaring up and crackling bright gold with pure heat and intensity - but be careful not to let the fire get too hot or burn too much! with this much energy in play it can be tempting to just "see where it goes" but the energy of the knight of wands requires careful stewardship and determination.

often the knight of wands appears to announce a sudden job change, a move, or a rearranging epiphany about the self. within the personality of the querent, the knight illustrates qualities of fearlessness, eagerness and ambition that can be of use when galloping through these changes, which, with the appearance of the knight of wands, are often inevitable. if symbolizing another person, the knight of wands is most likely someone decisive, impulsive, enthusiastic, passionate and decidedly self-governed. there is adventure represented here as well, the potential for sudden unexpected travel, or an unforeseen creative boon.

when the knight of wands appears, the message is that the querent keep moving forward at all costs - it is imperative. as there is no way to slow the fire, nor turn away from it, it must be guarded, maintained, and tended carefully but swiftly, and with little heed to anything else. in other words: be brave, and prioritize.

KNIGHT OF WANDS, REVERSED

the knight of wands has a bad side: aggressive, hasty, self-centered, unreliable, a fire that burns too hot and too fast, leaving nothing but ashes behind. this can be an undesired job change (they call it getting fired for a reason) or a situation that brings about significant anger. it can also be a warning to the querent to cool off before they do something regrettable. if representing an individual within the querent's life, the knight of wands reversed is a person to be careful around: their fire (often in the form of spite, sarcasm and aggression) is dangerous.

QUEEN OF WANDS

the queen of wands patiently observes the staff planted before her, as if willing a grafted branch to grow, directing all available energy to the creation of new life. backing her up in her garden ambitions are her traditional floral symbols, sunflowers, which represent joy, optimism and radiance.

i have long called the queen of wands "the mistress of creativity" because of the way she pops up so frequently for artists, representing a visit from the muses or a distinct connection to the sparkling link between creativity and spiritual fulfillment. traditionally, the queen of wands is understood to represent "the emotions transforming the will," or one's heart being aligned with one's actions, the feeling of doing what one truly loves. the queen of wands is very capable of manifesting her dreams, and is someone who must keep creativity flowing in order to experience regular happiness.

for the querent, the queen of wands speaks to the creative self in balance. she is the part of us that can stay busy but still be fully engaged with the world around us, free from stress, living in the moment - she is a reminder to continually engage with our creative side, to play with our surroundings and put good vibes into everything we do. her appearance in a reading is also an indication that we can have positive influence over those around us.

if representing a person in the querent's life, the queen of wands is someone bright-tempered, optimistic, helpful, open and inspiring.

QUEEN OF WANDS, REVERSED

the queen of wands reversed is a creative spirit blunted, an enthralling project interrupted, a frustrated energy with no opportunity for release. this card can appear when we have pushed ourselves too hard, when we have been providing inspiration for everyone but ourselves, when we have let ourselves down or failed to believe in ourselves. it can also stand in for someone who is tempestuous, tyrannical, angry or a bully. sometimes the queen of wands reversed indicates that we have lost faith in ourselves, that our self-confidence is low. again, creativity is the golden key that frees us from this prison. anything can be an act of creativity if we approach it with the right mindset.

KING OF WANDS

our king sits, as if in meditation, fixated on a wand that floats
above both hands. he is, as we can immediately see, capable of
great magic. whereas the preceding cards represent bringing
our ideas and creations into the world, the king of wands
represents, in some ways, bringing the world to his ideas and
creations. he is a powerfully persuasive figure, in some ways
aligned with the magician, because he possesses great power
and can change the world around him for the better.

what are you waiting for? the king of wands arriving in a
reading often suggests that you are faced with a once-in-a-

81

lifetime opportunity, a place to prove yourself, a chance to shine. the king of wands is confident, headstrong, and motivated by his ideals. he is certain his heart is in the right place, and if he appears as a representation of the querent, it is a sign that your heart is in the right place too. you know what you need, what you want, and how far you are willing to go to get there. It is no coincidence that his face in our deck is leonine - the king of wands is associated with the astrological sign of leo, natives born under which can be loving, generous, altruistic and inspiring if they are in balance.

If representing another person, the king of wands is someone self-assertive, daring, compassionate, idealistic and aware of his own power and influence - often someone with great philanthropic drive, someone who wishes to change the world. i call this card, sometimes "the patron saint of the activist." his powerful belief in what is right gives him all the energy he needs to accomplish his goals.

KING OF WANDS, REVERSED

selfishness, arrogance, thriving in disharmony, misuse of power - the king of wands reversed can represent a truly grim aspect of humanity (i often see him appear to represent totalitarian attitudes or the behavior of some people unfairly granted power over others - the king of wands is much like a cop or soldier, where in his upright position he strives to do good from his place of authority, and in a reversed position he can be really, truly tyrannical). he pops up like this when we are being intolerant, unnecessarily combative, when we are obsessed with our own correctness, or when we react without compassion - or when we are dealing with someone who displays those behaviors. focus on logic and on love. don't get caught in a burning building, whether that burning building is a senseless conflict, a manipulative dynamic, or a power struggle.

these little vessels, made of wood or clay or glass or even carved from stone, contain the whole world of feeling. the cups represent our emotions and intuition, our blood and our tears, the tenderest parts of us, as well as the truly passionate parts. they also, in times past, were associated with the clergy, with those who offered up their hearts to the realms of religion and mysticism, or to a higher power. they swirl up feelings of a spiritual nature then, as well: of transmutation, transfiguration, and transcendence. remember that "passion" comes from a root word meaning "to suffer" and that "compassion" therefore means "to suffer with." when we open our hearts to others (friends, family, lovers) we make the agreement to suffer with them. and within suffering can be found the pearls of truest wisdom.

but of course they can also represent martyrdom and fantasy. we need water to survive, but the well can be poisoned or it can flood us, wash us away. bear in mind that the lessons illuminated by the suit of cups are almost always lessons of emotional boundaries.

the cups are associated with the element of water, and with summertime, and with the transitional age between adolescence and adulthood. they correspond with the water signs in astrology: cancer, scorpio and pisces.

if a reading is predominantly cups, it may indicate that emotions are running high and that the potential for emotional fulfillment is very significant - though if many of the cups cards are reversed or blocked, it can signal that emotional events may be overwrought or overdramatized, or that a person may have numbly withdrawn from emotions entirely in an attempt to remain neutral and/or independent. depending on the other cards in the reading, a cups-heavy spread can represent an emotional breakthrough (or breakdown). there may be much processing to do. maybe a lot of crying. definitely some real gritty honesty, and probably some degree of devotional activities: praying if you are the type for such things and gardening, charitable works and gentle self-care if you aren't.

possible though, too, that all acts of love are acts of prayer if they are also acts of truth.

ACE OF CUPS

as the penultimate card of the emotional heart, the ace of cups
represents the center of your feelings in their absolute purest
state. there is a balanced mix of emotional and spiritual
components contained herein, having to do with both personal
fulfillment and depth of experience, which can naturally lead to
having a greater influence on the world around you. historically
a card of religious ecstasy, the ace of cups arrives in a reading
when we are being inundated by new or overwhelming
emotions - perhaps when we are falling in love, finding or
rediscovering a spiritual path, surrendering to forgiveness, or
otherwise opening up to truth in a way that changes us forever.

this is a card of innocence, divine purity and fearlessly opening the heart. sometimes there is no other way to live than to feel like one is spilling over and sloshing bright sparkling tears of reverence into the future.

don't be afraid to open. great potency is found here. traditionally this card is associated with the holy grail and represents your heart in its most pure and true state. for guidance, consider yourself as a child, and ask how you might have gone forward.

ACE OF CUPS, REVERSED

gentle, gentle. ace of cups reversed is a challenge to our sense of ourselves and our knowledge of our own truth. often it represents a situation in which a person is giving too much of themselves, either to another individual or to a life circumstance. it is an outpouring of emotion that is just "too much," too torrential, a flood, a disaster. be cautious and rein yourself in.

TWO OF CUPS

people are often so happy to overturn the lovers in a reading, without realizing everything that the lovers can contain: complexity, challenge, revelation, life-altering decision, ego death.

but here, here is the real "lord of love," as the gnostics call the card: surely one of the most romantic and emotionally vibrant of the tarot cards. two of cups represents a unification of souls, most often a romantic or intimate partnership. it can also be a deep and trusting friendship or other alliance, but it is one you give your whole heart to. you can call the two of cups a representation of the heart making a vow: the simultaneous selfishness/unselfishness of committed love. we are selfish because we depend on someone else; we are selfless because they depend on us too. ideally, we take balanced turns, as the monsters here are doing: one stands guard over the other as it rests. in due time, they will shift their roles.

when the two of cups arrives in a reading, it suggests that intimate relationships are in focus, that the time is ripe for cultivating, cherishing and honoring these closest bonds. who is your ride or die? who would you do anything for? what role do these relationships play in your life? how honest are they and how can you dedicate yourself to them more fully? alchemically, the two of cups is associated with unification, with true surrender. bear that in mind as you proceed.

TWO OF CUPS, REVERSED

an uncomfortable disparity, one partner more interested than the other, dissolution of friendship, one person looking for similarities while the other looks for differences: two of cups reversed is a lose-lose. it can represent the anguish that comes after a breakup, or the crisis that precedes it, but either way the message is clear: the querent must dedicate more of their energy to their original and most potent relationship - the relationship one has with oneself.

THREE OF CUPS

mirthful celebration, affirming friendship, warm reunions and celebration - these sentiments float in with the warm phosphorescent tide of the three of cups. this is a very sociable energy, vibrant and nourishing, giving you the opportunity to forget the cares of the world and just float. there is an easy, joyful vitality to be found in the right social situations. the monsters in this card are gentle and they kind of look like manatees, which is a good representation, as the three of cups contains within its mysteries the ability to soften one's heart and be nothing but optimistic and open. you've got to be careful, of course, lest something injure you - but you also got your crew, and you can count on taking care of each other.

looking at this card from a qabalistic perspective, we see that it is "binah in briah" or "the understanding of creation." what this means is that great feeling when we are in the present, feeling very loved and happy, and we realize that this, yes this, is what life is all about: this simplicity, this ease, this splendid happiness, this just plain living.

THREE OF CUPS, REVERSED

quit partying so hard. seriously. you think you're chasing the dragon but really the dragon is devouring you from the feet up because you are always out, always distracted, always hunting around, full of f.o.m.o., hungry and thirsty and spending too much money on drinks.

or maybe this is just a metaphor, maybe you have avoided the insincere party murk so often illuminated by the three of cups reversed. your emotions are probably still very muddy. some time alone might clarify them.

FOUR OF CUPS

the foliage in the four of cups card traditionally represents the bodhi tree, where the buddha waited im/patiently to disconnect his heart from the larger world. there's a dissatisfaction inherent in the four of cups, a boredom and a restlessness and oftentimes too a judgmentalism, an apathy, a sneering. wanting to be outside of or better than the sloppy old world, full of all its feelings and confusion. wanting to withdraw, and then because you are waiting and still, the vines grow over you and you are stuck, stuck, and you cannot decide which cup to drink from and even if you could - can you still move?

it is time to wake, to stir, to shake off what binds, what keeps you from truth. four of cups is about what happens when we try to escape our hearts - stasis. but stasis is an unnatural thing and cannot last without putrefaction setting in. so we must keep moving. we must drink from the cups we are offered, we must engage with our world or suffer the consequences.

FOUR OF CUPS, REVERSED

a four of cups reversed indicates that the querent is actively struggling with what has bound them: maybe a trauma or an emotionally challenging or unfulfilling upbringing, or a period of isolation or loneliness...it can feel like you are bound to it and it to you, but really you just need to grieve. try letting yourself cry. spill those wretched cups and keep moving.

FIVE OF CUPS

how much can a person hurt? how much loss can one being weather? how much trauma must an individual overcome? how lost in sorrow can we get ourselves, and how did the maps stop making sense? five of cups is all about the isolation of individual sadness, the intense solitude of grief or loss, despair or regret. it is focusing on the spilled cups, mourning what seeps away in the wake of something precious being broken. it is the memory of the dead haunting us, it is the echoes of past hurts stealing us from sleep, it is a belief that we are as broken or as empty as the cups before the monster in this card. the trick here, the secret treasure that the five of cups brings us, is to remember the full cups, the ones waiting for us when we finish with our grief. mourn not too long, dear one. there is still brightness in the world.

peony has even chosen to depict more full cups than this card traditionally has: usually there are three spilled and two full, but little monsters tarot takes an optimistic approach. perhaps you should try it too! remember that gratitude practices actually change your brain. what is one thing you can be thankful for?

FIVE OF CUPS, REVERSED

most frequently in my work as an interpreter of cards, i see five of cups reversed as a recovery card: signifying recognition or acceptance of the past, and a willingness to work toward a brighter and better future for oneself. the vision of those unseen full cups: knowing and believing in a glass-half-full world. you might be challenging a relationship with a dependency of some kind. if so, commendations are in order - but hard work, too, is still a part of this story. it is hard to dig through the muck of the past, but it is worth it for what you will be able to salvage.

SIX OF CUPS

ah, bright innocence! nostalgia, fond remembrances, poring
over old yearbooks, photographs, love letters, journals: wanting
to go back to a sweeter time, or a simpler one, or a time before
pain. if you have siblings or have maintained friendships from
childhood, they may be in focus now - same with old
relationships from long ago that seem gilded by the years that
have passed. the six of cups turns our thoughts toward the
joyousness and purity of the past, and encourages a fusion of
the innocent values of childhood with the demands and stresses
of the current world. in which ways could you be more like a
child? how can you uncover vulnerability, trust, kindness,

gentleness? how could these qualities, soft as flowers, serve you now? how could peace or a dedication to joy be your ally?

but also, be careful of escapism, of denial, of retreating...remember to hold innocence alongside boundaries, alongside being rational. a danger in six of cups is naivete, being too quick to forgive, or indulging in excessive wishful thinking. now is a very good time to think about parenting yourself. how would you best care for the childlike aspect of you? what boundaries do you need? in which ways can you be encouraged to play well with others, to be brave, to be generous?

SIX OF CUPS, REVERSED

dude, seriously, let it go. you know it's time. the past is gone and it ain't never coming back. that relationship that ended is over; that embarrassment was something you suffered years and years ago; the abuse you survived is in the past now; that missed opportunity will not come again; the dreams you had for yourself when you were 6 or 17 or 31 are not meant to be - but whatever past thing it is that you are focused on, the time has come to shake it off and get with the present moment. because you are robbing yourself of powerful joy by getting bogged down in old expectations and beliefs. you watch from the sidelines of your own past as life rushes by. take a deep breath and get over it. life is waiting.

SEVEN OF CUPS

here is the murky world of emotional possibility, of illusions, of fantasies and daydreams. the querent who is faced with the seven of cups is often a person who can foresee every possible outcome of any situation they are facing. this is the person who, when faced with a potential move or a new relationship or job opportunity, becomes inundated with all the variables: all the joy, all the strife, all the fear, all the triumph, anything that could be possible - often becoming so very dazzled by all that possibility that there is very little forward motion. there is an actual "castle in the sky" here. anyone with seven of cups placed prominently would be advised to follow the teachings of the six of cups preceding it: focus on the present, settle into the moment, and accept things as they come. we cannot predict the whole of the world, and if we try, we lose ourselves.

seven of cups is also a card about wishes and temptations, of juicy imaginings of what certain opportunities might mean, of heightened expectations that can lead only to disappointment. all that glitters is not gold, and those with such high expectations have hopes that shatter when dropped from such a height. so strive to stay humble, keep your feet on the ground, and accept the cup that is offered.

SEVEN OF CUPS, REVERSED

the seven of cups reversed is often about a fog clearing, or about breaking through a delusion. finally, things have come clear! the temptation wasn't worth it, the idea couldn't hold water, the daydream has proven to be just that...and now, even as you wrangle with disappointment and disillusionment, you may finally be able to explore the world from a position of greater truth. you may also have been caught in a lie, or realized that you've been hiding something about yourself from the world or from your closer relationships. now is a time of practicality, of honesty, of simplicity. avoid complications and pursue the simplest truths you know.

EIGHT OF CUPS

and suddenly, it is time to go. time to walk away.

the eight of cups almost always signifies a time of withdrawal and hermitude, a stepping down or a stepping away. there comes a point in all of our lives when we must turn away from what we have so far accomplished, when we must retreat and return unto ourselves to gain deeper information. the querent may well be realizing that what they thought might bring them joy, satisfaction, and fulfillment just isn't quite cutting it.

the eight of cups typically arrives in our lives when we have everything that we thought we wanted, but we realize unequivocally that we need something more, something else, something deeper, something real. there is still more to seek. there is disappointment here: of course there is. how many hours, days, months, years you may have dedicated to a situation that is simply not panning out. there is also instability: where to now, my friend?

remember all that you have done. recognize the lessons. breathe deep and then step back.

EIGHT OF CUPS, REVERSED

relinquish, relinquish, relinquish. the past is ruling you. your old dreams inform the self too much. be wary, though, of leaving too much. you may want to give everything away, burn all of your bridges, when all you need is a little time to process. don't be hasty, don't run away. trouble with intimacy may be afoot: is there room to open more?

NINE OF CUPS

my nickname for this card has always been "the merchant of happiness." here we see someone who truly loves what they do, and does what they love. there is deep satisfaction here, a sense of worldly bliss. the whole world with all of its glory opens before you like a flower, and you can enjoy each moment for what it is: a precious gift. just like the monster easefully holding up four full cups, you are able to balance many things and experiences and unify them into one human story.

nine of cups often comes up as a symbol of a life well lived, either as a goal or a realization. now is the time to drink deep, to live boldly, to experience all that makes life worthwhile. do not shy away from your own power, your own potential.

NINE OF CUPS, REVERSED

arrogance, greed, entitlement. the querent is good but not perfect, and must be wary of thinking themselves so. nine of cups reversed can be an emotional high-horse, the belief that one has all the answers. it can also indicate that your boundaries are not as broad as you think them: be cautious not to press yourself into overindulgence.

TEN OF CUPS

welcome, friend, to the house of heaven.

now immersed in deep trust, this monster balances a rainbow of emotion above them, creating a bower of feeling beneath which to celebrate the preciousness of human experience. the appearance of the ten of cups shows that the focus in on deep harmony, on profound trust, and on honoring the bonds of the heart. having completed the full cycle of the emotional cups journey, the ten emerges as one who can hold all manner of experience as an array both useful and mysterious. there is a wonderful sense of completion here, of acceptance, of openness.

all the world is open before you, and there is no reason to fear. perhaps everything in life has a reason, an origin, and a grace, and perhaps we open our hearts only to bear witness to this glory.

follow your heart: it knows the way to wholeness.

TEN OF CUPS, REVERSED

it may be that things are falling apart. it may be that something you believed in was an illusion. it may be that the promised water was just a mirage. it may be that you were lied to. ten of cups reversed is a raw and arduous time, a time of confusion and the hard awareness of the limitations of those you love. you may be finding disappointment at every turn. you may also be living in a way that is not aligned with your own truth. ask yourself for the primary ethics of your own heart, and then strive to live by those rules.

CHILD OF CUPS

this is, by far, the most youthful of the tarot cards, and in some ways the most pure and joyous. the child of cups represents one whose heart is as open as a newborn star. turning up in a reading, this card can herald good news, a brand new start, or a powerful change in one's emotional trajectory. there is such a sweetness here: this person or aspect of the self is all about dreaminess, gentleness, hope, and virtue. this is a symbol for the most sensitive and delicate part of ourselves, of everyone, the childlike heart.

use your compassion. believe in your dreams. have faith, and above all, be open. the child of cups is powerfully receptive, interested in receiving, in learning, in trusting. it is ok to be sentimental, to be nostalgic, to be gentle. vulnerability is also strength.

CHILD OF CUPS, REVERSED

the child of cups reversed is a temper tantrum: selfish, short-sighted, and emotionally volatile. taking things personally, refusing to look beyond the self, haranguing others when we don't get our way. the child of cups reversed is melancholy and moody, and may lack self-love. this can be dangerous because of course it can spill over like an upturned cup and we can end up abusing those connections we hold dearest. careful with your temper - your heart deserves love and satisfaction, but not without bounds.

KNIGHT OF CUPS

listen, listen, listen, to the poem of the heart. the knight of cups knows every line, has it memorized, can improvise in a moment. the knight of cups is sensual, romantic, powerfully emotional, profound. there may be flirtation, seduction or romantic interest sparking blue the air around you. there may be a deepening of feeling, a sense of diving for pearls. the knight of cups is a good listener with a warm and open heart, who is unafraid of truth, or so it seems: the knight of cups knows depth like no one else, but beware the shifting of the tide.

because, you see, the knight of cups also often represents illusion, fantasy, and escapism, and fundamentally, the knight is also self-involved and led entirely by their own heart. so, just like the moon guides the tides, there is a bit of the coming in and then receding in the knight of cups, some inconstancy governing the emotional mood, because while the knight of cups is capable of great closeness, they are also capable of great distance. you may be faced with a person who gets very close and then recedes with little warning, or someone aloof and at a distance who suddenly seeks intimacy.

associated with the sign of pisces, the knight of cups is slippery as a fish. emotion is unpredictable and irrational, in ourselves and in others. if we dive too deep, we just might drown. best learn to swim.

KNIGHT OF CUPS, REVERSED

if it seems too good to be true, it probably is. knight of cups reversed can often represent a trap, a manipulative situation or an emotional puppet-master. the knight of cups reversed is one of the more dismal and dangerous personae represented in the tarot: a situation, relationship or person with much appeal and glamor - but when the truth is revealed, the illusion shattered, it is often a situation of profound lies and potential for tragedy. if knight of cups comes up reversed in your reading, especially in regards to a relationship, be careful to listen only to your own voice. your intuition knows the way, but it is a delicate thing, and revealing too much can make you dangerously vulnerable.

QUEEN OF CUPS

if you've ever had the experience of being gently and caringly listened to, until a weight lifts from your heart like a bird taking flight, then you already know the queen of cups. nurturing, kind, receptive and intuitive, the queen of cups knows the heart and is unafraid of its depths. she is tranquil and connected, fair and loving. the queen of cups is known in elemental terms as "the emotions strengthen the emotions" - understanding, relating and achieving intimacy give the queen her power in the world.

it may be that there is someone in your life who is acting as your mirror, or it may be an aspect of yourself that is emerging, offering peace, grace and understanding to those around you, or to a part of yourself that has been neglected and unheard. sometimes the queen of cups lacks common sense, or can be dreamy or vague, but her powerful connection with the subconscious guides her so that she becomes a beacon of loving-kindness.

there is a song of the self that we all know by heart. the queen of cups knows it too. go ahead and give a listen.

QUEEN OF CUPS, REVERSED

there is a worry here that you may have become disconnected from yourself, that there might be an abundance of deception or delusion in your life. often when the queen of cups appears in a reversed position it can indicate that your emotions are running away from you, and that your delightful but confused heart is getting the better of you in certain situations. beware gullibility. beware trusting when trust has not been earned. and be certain, too, that you are not the culprit, that you are not the one to blame for this strange and murky brew.

KING OF CUPS

here is a master of his emotion. very emotionally balanced and in control, kind but not naive, giving but not self-sacrificing, understanding but not enabling, the king of cups knows that the heart is the key, but he also knows how to protect it and all of the secrets it can access.

if the king of cups turns up in your reading, it can signify a person who is very adept at balancing emotions, or it could show that you yourself are now learning this skillful balance. king of cups is associated with the sign of scorpio, those deep divers who know intimately the least illuminated spaces in the human psyche; those who love, without remorse, the darker corners of the human heart. but the king of cups does not dwell in misery or loss, in grief or anger, but rather rises above them and learns to translate their intricate calligraphy into a poetry of the soul.

above all else, the king of cups is the card of emotional management, of knowing the limits and boundaries of the heart. now would be an excellent time to examine where those boundaries are. do they need adjustment? do they need reinforcement? do they need to be tested?

you are powerful beyond a doubt. you know what you need.

KING OF CUPS, REVERSED

ugh, gross. watch out for this creepy energy, in yourself or in others. king of cups reversed is a toxic, controlling, emotionally abusive energy that runs the risk of seeping into every aspect of your life. high drama! the best thing you can do is withdraw from these ugly, repugnant vibes. whatever the king of cups reversed is representing, be it work, love, or family: a little time away to detox the heart is called for. just back it up. trust me.

COINS

the coins (also called pentacles or disks in other decks)
represent the element of earth and the material world, the
tangible stuff. i always say that they rule over our houses, our
bodies, our time, our money and how we spend or use each of
these things. look for messages about home, health, livelihood,
and finances, and especially for information about time as a
tangible thing, an investment, a measurement, and a value.

the coins are associated with middle age, with maturity, with
adulthood and with all of the responsibilities therein. they are
also affiliated with the season of autumn, and indeed there's a
feeling of sacrifice and preparation about them sometimes: an
energetic preparation for the winter that comes through true
understanding your resources. taurus, virgo and capricorn all
fall under the rule of the coins, as do their standout qualities of
resourcefulness, pragmatism, materialism and comparative
analysis.

peony uses a five-petaled flower in the center of each coin, to tie
in the coins suit's connection to nature and to the natural world.
today, a lot of humans spend less time outdoors and less time
directly engaged with our physical bodies than most of our
ancestors did, and while there are of course positive aspects to
this, there are also arguably times when we might improve our
situation were we to simply take a walk, get some fresh air, look
at a flower, or feel our own heartbeat. the coins cards serve,
then, to remind us of our primal, physical, natural selves.

if there are a lot of coins turning up in a reading, it can be a sign
that there is a material-world opportunity presenting itself -
could be a business deal, a real estate venture or a contract of
some kind. it could also be that there is an emphasis being
placed on hearth or health and the happiness that can be gained
from each.

pay attention to the messages of the coins: they are arguably the most direct and straightforward of the cards, though people sometimes have a tendency to overlook their simple and down-to-earth information in favor or something more grand or esoteric. it is advisable to remember that we do, in fact, live in a material world.

ACE OF COINS

gnostics call this card "the root of the powers of the earth." and here it is, coming up like a mushroom from the ground, abundantly surrounded by proliferating greenery. the flowers that peony has drawn hint at dandelions, an herb whose root is has been used for thousands of years for grounding and detoxification, for putting the physical body back into primal balance - and that's what the ace of coins is about too.

perhaps most primally, the ace of coins illustrates a profound desire to engage with the physical world in a more holistic way. this card often comes up when a querent is experiencing an illness that has drastically affected their physical well-being, when they are living with chronic pain, body dysphoria, or trauma which negatively influences their ability to be fully "in their body." nonetheless, the desire is there: to feel the wind on your skin, the grass beneath your feet, the sun on your back, to smell the flowers and hear the birds singing.

but fear not! even where there is this great hunger and longing, there is opportunity here too. when the ace of coins appears, i have been known to murmur "well, ante up," because the ace of coins is showing that it is time. time to take that risk, to begin anew. time to be honest about what you need for your own survival. time to move to a new home or new city or new school or new career path, to engage with the body differently, to take control of your health, to dive into your own power.

ACE OF COINS, REVERSED

you know the saying "stop while you're ahead"? well, it's a little late for that maybe, but you could try stopping before you are further behind. the ace of coins reversed suggests that maybe you are slogging along on a project or path or plan that is in danger of collapsing - and dogged determination and perseverance probably won't make it any better, unfortunately. we sometimes like to believe that just throwing ourselves and our energies at something will make it successful. sometimes, as here, that is just not the case. give in, give up, and take some time for yourself.

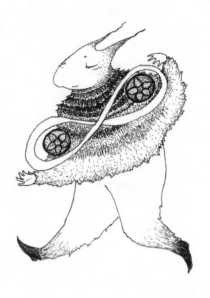

TWO OF COINS

gotta strike that balance, yo! the two of coins just can't stop /
won't stop. in some ways the two of coins represents life itself,
and the permanence of change. indeed, the esoteric title for the
card is "the lord of harmonious change," because everything is
always cycling, cycling, like the mythical ouroboros, the snake
eating its own tail, the looping infinite lemniscate that takes a
brief vacation from the major arcana to turn up here in the
material world, illuminating the spiritual necessity of material
world balance.

more simply put: sometimes taking care of business is the most spiritually attuned thing you can do. two of coins suggests that there might be a way to just go with the flow and avoid falling into the pitfall of the "i'm so busy, i'm so stressed" culture that we love to play with these days. there might be a way to do all that you need and not a bit more, not a bit less. be very, very, very clear where you want to invest your energy and do not falter: it is very easy to interrupt this flow.

TWO OF COINS, REVERSED

whoa, dude, take it easy. you have waaaaay too many irons in the fire, and it is likely making you undependable, incompetent, forgetful, and unreliable - and maybe irritable, sleepless and frustrated too! the two of coins reversed almost always represents someone who has taken on way too many things and needs to drop some burdens for their own health's sake.

THREE OF COINS

things come to fruition in the three of coins, called "the lord of material works."

much hard work has been done, many plans overseen, many hours have been toiled through, and now all begins to coalesce. quite frequently we see the three of coins appear as a symbol that the querent has achieved a material world success: a new job, completed project, or other triumph. but my personal nickname for this card has always been "the apprentice." some people insist that the eight of coins is the card of an apprenticeship, but i would say that's more like a journeyman.

the three of coins shows the exhilaration of an early accomplishment: what we see is merely the first achievement in a series of great works to come. rounding a corner of knowledge: what else is to come to pass in the near future? what is your next move? what is the next step? who can you best learn from, and how?

three of coins is a symbol of completion, yes, but it is also a sign to continue. this path is beautiful; this path blooms. gather yourself, humble yourself, and keep walking.

THREE OF COINS, REVERSED

maybe loosen your grasp. maybe forgive others and yourself for shortcomings. three of coins reversed is sometimes a headache of expectation, a boredom, a self-centeredness. i see this card most frequently where teamwork has been abandoned, and the querent may take oneself to be the most important part of a complicated puzzle.

remember: everything we ever accomplish is accomplished with the help and oversight of others. we are never alone.

FOUR OF COINS

i like to call this card "the banker." here is somebody who has it
all figured out, who understands worldly success and financial
boon and makes all the necessary steps to secure their material
world future: the lord of earthly power. the earth element is
associated with the number 4, and here we have what might be
called "the earth of earth," the element of earth within the
concept of earth. there is groundedness, of course. there can also
be an obsession with the material world, with success, with
money, with the body. and an obsession with the material world
runs the risk of closing out the other worlds: the spiritual, the
emotional, the creative.

security is a tricky thing. on the one hand, we may be triumphing at our ability to survive, to succeed. on the other, we can become stagnant.

control, too, plays a part here. it can be exhilarating to feel like you are in control - but how does it feel if you are not?

pay close attention to issues of work and livelihood when the four of coins makes itself known in a reading. is your job liberating you or holding you back? what do you truly want and require from your livelihood?

FOUR OF COINS, REVERSED

possessiveness doesn't look pretty on anyone, nor greed. there is a concern when the four of coins turns up reversed that a person may be acting petty, suspicious, or overly controlling. a great fear is here, behind all of these actions or impulses: a fear of losing something precious. turning over the four of coins reversed is a good indicator that it may be time to find new ways of feeling secure, ways that exist beyond money, reputation, or the body.

FIVE OF COINS

five of coins represents a time of instability, fear, loss, poverty, isolation. yet within the card, especially here in peony's rendition, there is great hope - because compassion exists beyond all struggles of the material world. in spite of any lack in the material, we can find ways to compensate in the emotional and spiritual realms. we care for one another, and that accounts for the greatest riches in all the world.

it may be that you feel worthless, unwanted, shunned, rejected or injured by the world at large. this card especially relates to oppression on a sociopolitical scale: to issues of racism, classism, homophobia, transphobia, misogyny and so forth. but even amidst our trials and suffering, there is a glimmer of hope, just as was uncovered at the bottom of pandora's box: and that hope is basic kindness.

because there are always people who want to help. it is just a matter of finding them.

do your best to get your material world affairs in order, but let others help. because they want to.

FIVE OF COINS, REVERSED

no need to be so stoic. no one in this world is alone, not even you.

five of coins reversed is one of the biggest indicators to me that a person may be falling into isolationist self-pity, the idea that no one wants them, no one loves them, no one needs them.

this could not be further from the truth. it is essential to understand that there is a reason you were born. there is a special story only you can tell, and your job now is to get out there and tell it.

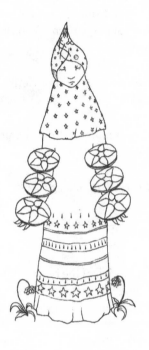

SIX OF COINS

what a careful balancing act! this monster so carefully measures what it can give, while flowers wilt at its feet. remember: if the coins represent our bodies, our money, our time - the six comes in to remind and reinforce lessons about exactly how much we can give, and also how much we can keep for ourselves.

have you been too stingy? too giving? too forward? too reserved? too open? too defensive? the six of coins interrogates all of these dichotomies, demanding to know how you spend your time and how you keep yourself balanced. there is an african proverb: "never trust a naked man who is offering you a shirt." this is especially relevant here. we cannot trust love that comes from those who do not love themselves. we cannot rely on those who fail to meet their own needs.

many associate this card with charity and charitable works - as well they should! sometimes the message of the six of coins is as simple as to say that a querent has been giving of themselves in a beautiful way. but sometimes it suggests that more giving is necessary, and sometimes it indicates that too much has been offered. what is most important here is the balance, the discernment.

you know how on an airplane they say you have to put on your own oxygen mask before you help someone else with theirs? that's the six of coins.

SIX OF COINS, REVERSED

boundaries, friend. set your boundaries. be very careful about lending, getting into debt, making agreements you are not ready for.

six of coins reversed indicates you are being asked for more than you can give. be very, very, very careful. think back on the lessons of the cards preceding: if you are not materially secure and sound, you cannot help anyone. so be cautious. don't be afraid to say no.

SEVEN OF COINS

time to see how your garden has grown. time to evaluate. there
is a moment to rest and reflect now, and you have a unique
opportunity, a special moment, to take stock of all you have
accomplished, of everything you have done until now. i always
talk about this card as i would talk about a garden: you, the
gardener, have worked long and hard, you have tended many
rows and sown many seeds, hoed and weeded and harvested,
and now there is the harvest: where you can see what works,
what doesn't, what should be replanted, what should be
moved, what should change. what is getting enough light?

which crops produced the best results? what withered and required too much attention to be truly fruitful?

now is a time of making decisions. on the simplest level, this can be a purely physical decision, relating to the body: maybe you have realized a food allergy or sensitivity, or you have come to understand that there is a simple practice that would help you feel physically better each day. or it might relate to your career or academic path, or to your home life.

sometimes there is frustration or exhaustion coming in with this harvest. what's important to realize is that you have your future in mind, and you are nurturing it. if you trust yourself enough, you will make the right choices.

SEVEN OF COINS, REVERSED

whoa, this garden is weedy! overgrown with potential. sometimes we start projects with the best of intentions and just can't see them through, for whatever reason. procrastination is rampant with the seven of coins reversed, and so is feeling trapped in obligations that just don't serve us. don't be afraid to walk away from something that is not fruitful. sometimes the best thing you can do is let go.

EIGHT OF COINS

patience, patience. all will come to pass. the eight of coins
frequently turns up at a time when we feel we have done
everything we can and our work does not yet speak for itself. i
associated the eight of coins frequently with artists who are
doing all they can to produce and promote their work and have
not yet found the success they seek, but the qabalistic
intelligence associated with the eight of coins is called the
"perfect absolute intelligence." what that means is that all is as
it should be. there are no mistakes.

find reassurance here, in the product you carefully cradle in your hands. you know that your efforts are pure-hearted. if you can just be gentle with yourself, your destiny will unfold before you as it is intended.

EIGHT OF COINS, REVERSED

don't stand in your own way! eight of coins reversed indicates perfectionism, being overly cautious, resistance, self-doubt. this is likely a moment when you can accomplish great things, if you can just learn to step aside and relax. just let it happen, because it is all happening.

NINE OF COINS

enjoy this moment. you have earned it. this luxury, this beauty, this self-reliance, all of it belongs to you in this moment. things can change (and they surely will), but here we see a gorgeous time of contemplation, completion, fulfillment, the kind of moment we dream of. take your time with it. you have worked long and hard to achieve this, and you are deserving.

a project may be completed, a goal achieved, a sense of harmony dominates the senses. please, take the time to revel in it. this simple glory is the fruit of life.

a deception is afoot. you're feeling pressure to act like something you're not, and you're playing the role, but it is killing your spirit. there is no need to pretend, not really. the right people will always accept you as you are.

TEN OF COINS

completion. a story comes full circle, often a family story. historically, the ten of coins represented an inheritance or homecoming. that's accurate, to a point, but really we are talking about ancestral karmas here, genetic wealth or genetic disparity. sometimes the ten of coins suggests a health or money problem associated with one's family, a genetic disease or an old debt, but i have especially seen the ten of coins play out as a representation of one's familial legacy in sociopolitical terms. what does it mean to come from the family you came from? what do your origins tell you? how are you affected by your own history?

because the tens represent the completion of a cycle, it is important to ask yourself how you wish to carry your legacy forward. what will you take with you? what is most dear? what truly represents you as you are now?

TEN OF COINS, REVERSED

the most indicative card of family trouble. old stories haunting you, or new dramas unfolding. this can be within your family of origin or your larger chosen family or community. you may feel estranged or taken advantage of, or as if your loyalties are pulled in different directions. take things slowly. of course, this is always good advice, but here, especially, count carefully and think logically.

CHILD OF COINS

here is the very definition of precocious: someone patient, steady, and wise beyond their years, studious and mature, even in the midst of their own naivete. the child of coins is a gentle little genius, a wise but inexperienced person who does their very best. because of the material world indication of the coins, the child of coins often represents a person who has advanced suddenly in the world of business or academia, a person prepared but not quite qualified. this can, of course, be the querent, or someone close to them. either way, look for someone who has jumped into something they are not wholly prepared for but that they are passionate about nonetheless.

the earthy innocence of the child of coins will likely reward their earnest efforts. don't be too nervous: everyone was inexperienced at some time or another, and it takes risks to flourish.

sometimes, the appearance of the child of coins is a simple message about a new job or a new area of study, something blooming up from between the cracks in the asphalt, a determined thing, a bright and living force. nurture this thing, this new possibility. it is precious.

CHILD OF COINS, REVERSED

a brilliant student who refuses to do homework. a writer avoiding deadlines. a person with a glorious business proposal or workplace suggestion who lacks the wherewithal to make moves. a little encouragement is necessary here, a little boost in bravery. don't hide from glory - it is your birthright.

KNIGHT OF COINS

trustworthy, steadfast, responsible, analytical - the astrological sign of virgo at its best. there is a fastidious orderliness to the knight of coins, a predictability, and a font of trust in the world: trusting that if you do something carefully, cautiously, and conservatively, then good results will come from your efforts in due time.

the knight of coins, whether it represents you or someone close to you, is all about slow and steady winning the race. there is stamina here because the knight of coins knows the path so well. it is a way they have walked a thousand times, either in actuality or just in mental preparation for the task at hand. they can go and go and go and go, until the job is done, for perseverance is the name of the knight of coins' game, and because of this diligence there is a promise from the universe that they will succeed.

it may be time to take charge and see something through to its natural conclusion, or, if this card represents someone beloved to the querent, it may be time to cede to their expertise and tenacity. there may be stress associated with this time, but it will be worth it in the end, because the knight of coins has this in the bag, even if it might look like they don't.

KNIGHT OF COINS, REVERSED

stuck in a rut, life is boring, everything is rote and mundane. the knight of coins reversed has chosen their own prison and just sits there, obediently, even though the possibility of escape is near at hand. time to get free!

QUEEN OF COINS

here is the o.g. earth mama, the primordial nurturer, who best shows her love by feeding, tending, and care-taking. the queen of coins is practical, down-to-earth, subtle and prosperous. she is generous with her time and energy, sharing freely with those she loves, but she is also cautious and somewhat demure, or shy.

for now, the focus is on this gentle, easy sense of balance and integrity. sometimes the queen of coins represents a life situation: a job or project that is currently serving to bolster your spirits. other times she is a kind and serious friend or lover, supporting you from behind the scenes. or she can be a part of yourself, that gives generously from a seemingly bottomless well. financial generosity is a big part of the queen of coins, as are the gifts of food, touch and simple companionship. great comfort is here, a feeling of being at home in the world.

if there is anything to watch out for, it is the queen of coins' potential to be too timid, a pushover, someone who can be easily taken for granted. sometimes the simplest pleasures are worth much more than anything extravagant.

QUEEN OF COINS, REVERSED

if e'er there was a workaholic represented in the tarot, it would be here, in the queen of coins reversed. here the constant dedication of the queen becomes thwarted as she assigns all of her energy and focus to a menial and material task - the person who stays late at the office for no real reason, buries themselves in unnecessary busy work, loads up on extra assignments without necessity. what is it that you or your beloved is avoiding?

KING OF COINS

no one gives better advice than the king of coins. and luckily, no one enjoys giving it more than he. here is another nurturing, capable, serious figure emerging from the coins court: one who understands the struggles of the material world because he has lived them, and seeks to impart the wisdom he has gained through his own foibles and triumphs. look to the most experienced part of yourself, or a person in your life who is an unquestionable authority, when you see the king of coins appear in a reading.

stable, kind, and active, the king of coins has been called "the prince of the chariot of the earth." he understands. he knows how to get things done, and he will help, because it brings him a great sense of satisfaction. the mentor, the protector, the guide. the king of coins represents a wise choice, a reliable decision, a trustworthy guardian, the very ideal of a father figure, found in yourself or in someone close to you.

the king of coins has ultimate faith in you, and he takes great self-worth in governing and assisting you to your highest potential. how good it is to have this force of nature in your corner. success, with the king of coins at your side, is imminent.

KING OF COINS, REVERSED

excessively involved in affairs of the material world; too interested in money, sex, food, glamor. attached and stubborn, controlling, takes too much credit. a sleazy businessman type, a deification of worldly success that is ultimately empty.

the end, the air, the wind, the winter. traditionally called swords, peony has selected arrows to stand in for this final suit in the matter arcanum, which is associated with the mind, the mental landscape, logic, knowledge and thought, and with the air signs aquarius, gemini and libra.

they are also associated with, to some degree, suffering and death. it is true that the swords, or arrows, rule over the last years of life, the end of a seasonal cycle, over isolation and cold and thin high altitude wanderings. but this suit gets a bad rap, and a lot of books that you will read will say that a spread with a heavy emphasis on swords is a surefire sign that someone is really going through the wringer. i would argue that the same could be said for any of the suits, really. these cards in particular speak to the mental anguish and overstimulation that we so frequently experience, but they are no "worse" than any of the other cards.

in many ways, the arrows are the most zen of all the cards, or they have the potential to be, since in their best state they represent skillful mastery over the mind. if you see a lot of them crop up at once, meditation may be in order, or cognitive behavioral therapy, or very deliberately "changing your mind." an abundance of arrows can also represent a simple hunger for knowledge, or a new interest in the realms of philosophy, theology, or critique - or, i have noticed in the past few years, it can simply represent the state of being overstimulated by too much information. if the internet and advancing information technology was associated with any suit, it would surely be the arrows.

ACE OF ARROWS

you know the cartoon moment where the light bulb blinks on over somebody's head? that's ace of arrows territory.

here is a sudden breakthrough, a new idea, a bold innovation, a bright solution. quick wits, sharp logic, and all with such swiftness too! it is all coming in now, everything converging, all systems go. the ace of arrows is a symbol for a brilliant mind, shooting through the clouds going straight up to the pure atmosphere above and beyond. this is the card of rising above with a logical assessment or argument.

often the ace of arrows is about rallying around a strongly-held belief, finding the courage or resources to stand up for what you truly care about, using a sharp tongue efficiently to achieve justice or change. it can be about coming out, lodging a complaint against unfairness, giving testimony, or getting something off your chest that has weighed on you for far too long.

ACE OF ARROWS, REVERSED

the only thing is to beware of causing verbal or mental injury to yourself or others by moving too fast. the thrill of this intellectual empowerment is certain, but there is definitely some potential stress associated with this card, too. care should be taken to measure impulses against logic - because the aces always represent something that is just beginning, it can be that the ace of arrows represents a new idea or new way of thinking that seems perfect but has fatal flaws. watch your tongue, watch your thoughts, and don't be like icarus and fly too high is all i'm saying.

TWO OF ARROWS

i always associate this card with ancient traditional rites of
passage that once occurred all over the world around the age of
puberty. it is no surprise that peony chose an antlered monster
to portray this moment of indecision, this stasis, as most
antlered creatures go through cycles where they lose their old
pair and replace them with new ones. these growth cycles can
be painful and they require patience and diligence, just like the
two of arrows.

usually, this card marks a period of indecision, vagueness,
confusion, or overwhelm. it feels like a choice must be made,

but it also feels like you don't have all the information you need. it can feel like you are very isolated and on your own, but there is also a feeling of giddy self-reliance - how wonderful it is to be able to depend on yourself.

with the arrows representing death and the end of cycles, i often think of the two of arrows as representing the death of childhood: there is a loss of innocence, maybe even a loss of faith, and many choices to be made, but there is also great relief at being able to look within and make a decision for yourself. heed your intuition! it will lead the way.

TWO OF ARROWS, REVERSED

here is a situation where you have made a decision, then gone back on it, then made the decision again, and it is exhausting you, all this back and forth. maybe there is pressure to make a clear choice, or maybe you are just forcing yourself before you know you are ready.

as difficult as this can be, two of arrows often demands that you make a choice and stick to it. draw straws if you must, or use a pendulum or see a fortune-teller. but just decide and stay with what you choose, because you are losing touch with yourself in the struggle.

THREE OF ARROWS

this is some romeo and juliet business right here. so much heartbreak. while the three of arrows is not exclusively associated with romantic heartbreak, that is its most common dominion (in our culture at least). because, remember: the arrows represent the mind - so here is the three, which is associated with the triangle, and with the element of fire, and so we have a fire of the mind, an obsession. and the three of arrows is an obsession with pain.

a relationship that is continually causing agony. a breakup that you cannot stop thinking about. a rejection that you have allowed to color your self-perception. a fixation on an ex's social media accounts, maybe?

the only proper answer to the three of arrows is to turn your thoughts elsewhere. get your mind off of things. focus on something else. otherwise, the misery will continue.

THREE OF ARROWS, REVERSED

very rarely do i read reversed cards as the true "opposite" of their upright positions, but the three of arrows may come the closest. when i see this card reversed, it usually means that the querent has gone through some of the agony and heartbreak indicated by the three of arrows, but that they have triumphed over the quagmire of sorrow and learned from the pain, that they are doing a good job of moving on and moving through. it doesn't necessarily mean that everything is perfect, but it does mean that they are processing grief as efficiently as it can be processed.

FOUR OF ARROWS

sometimes when i see this card in someone's reading, i just want to start singing them lullabies straightaway, just skip the rest of the reading and let them lay down for a nap. the four of arrows is a surefire sign that somebody needs some r&r, that it is time to slow down and recuperate before the next wave of life challenges arrives.

it can be really hard to just sit still and rest. there's so much pressure to be doing things all the time; it can be almost embarrassing to take time to zone out, or nap, or goof off. but when you actually look at the habits of the world's most successful humans, you'll see that they are all really good at taking breaks. taking breaks is essential, and the four of arrows arrives to let you know it is time to take one of those breaks.

traditionally, the card shows an armored knight at rest surrounded by weapons, suggesting that preparing for an impending battle is at hand - but there is another, deeper message, which is one of healing. it may be that the querent has recently passed through a difficult time, or is pushing themselves too hard and is in desperate need of a break. many healers agree that the greatest threat to our health is stress, and that the greatest antidote to stress just might be stillness.

FOUR OF ARROWS, REVERSED

overstimulation to avoid emotional depth - like reading internet news at 3 a.m. when you know you should be sleeping. like checking facebook because you are lonely. mock rest: you might be lying down but your mind is going wild. now is more important than ever to practice mindfulness and focus techniques. quiet, quiet, quiet. find tranquility and revel in it.

FIVE OF ARROWS

who would need all of those arrows? why so many when you only need one to take a clear shot? five of arrows signifies a time of suspicion or lack of clarity about which thoughts are truly essential. there is often an air of tension or hostility - you may feel under attack or overly scrutinized, and you are beefing up your defenses in a way that may not be wholly necessary. i always warn people when this card comes up that carrying so many weapons is likely only going to hurt one person in the end: you. there is too much ambition here, too much lust for victory.

we all get hurt sometimes, and the five of arrows almost certainly indicates some level of personal injury, but what becomes important is keeping mental perspective, not jumping to conclusions or taking things too far in a conflict. avoid overextending yourself. if you are having a conflict with a friend, with coworkers, or with family, don't let your thoughts race ahead of you. keep things calm and simple, and find a way to focus on facts, not fantasy.

FIVE OF ARROWS, REVERSED

in a reversed position, the five of arrows shows that the querent is ready to give in, to relinquish, to forgive, but doesn't quite know how. because of the arrows' rulership over communication, the indication of this card may well be that honesty is the best policy. ask for a sit-down and try as best you can to open your heart. tell the truth. keep it simple. lay down your arms.

SIX OF ARROWS

escape is possible. the problems you face now may seem
especially difficult, even insurmountable, but the six of arrows
promises that you can evade them with enough presence of
mind. all possible shots have been fired, and none have stuck.
there is great regret here - the monster doesn't want to have to
go, but there is no other choice. often the six of arrows arrives
when it is time to leave a relationship, job, or living situation
that has become undeniably untenable. because of the
awareness that the arrows represents, you can no longer deny
your own needs, your own truth. while it is sad, it is time to go.

take heart, though: the six of arrows is nicknamed "the lord of earned success." what this means is that this difficult transition will be rewarded in time. your survival is your responsibility, but your destiny is under your control now. remember the russian proverb: "pray to god, but row for shore."

SIX OF ARROWS, REVERSED

your past keeps circling around to interrupt your progress. my unfortunate nickname for the six of arrows reversed is "the p.t.s.d. card." no matter your best efforts, thoughts and patterns from a painful chapter of your past return and hinder your evolution. it could be flashbacks or longstanding behavioral issues that threaten you, or it could be an actual person or situation: a legal predicament or an individual who will not leave you alone.

take necessary action. make an appointment with a therapist. investigate a restraining order. sign up for some meditation classes. find some herbs for anxiety. whatever it takes - you have likely had the solution flit into your mind but have had trouble taking action. however, if you don't take action, this situation will continue to plague you.

SEVEN OF ARROWS

well hello, trickster.

this is a card of secrets, of deception, of mental knavery. the sevens are complex cards, powerful and intense, but also deeply conflicted. here, the seven appearing in the realm of the mind represents the continued stress of lying or maintaining deceit. there is an element of trying to get away with something or pull something off without having others catch on. this could be something as minimal as trying to get a professional position without all the necessary requirements (and who hasn't fudged a résumé once or twice?) but it could be as large as maintaining

an infidelity or keeping a damaging secret that can cause
significant injury or trial for someone close to you.

the seven of arrows has a certain danger in it, which is the
danger of tricking oneself. beware of justifying actions that you
know in the core of yourself are wrong. beware "the lord of
unstable effort." this is one that can certainly come back to bite
you in the end.

SEVEN OF ARROWS, REVERSED

denial, shiftiness, self-delusion. willfully ignoring evidence. it
may be that someone else is deceiving you, and you know it,
but you make excuses for them. why? often all that the seven of
arrows reversed needs is an admission of guilt, or an
acknowledgement of wrongdoing. remember how
rumpelstiltskin falls to pieces when the queen finds out his
name? if we call things by their names we can have power over
them.

EIGHT OF ARROWS

one of my favorite revelations with tarot ever came when one of my teachers pulled this card for me. uneasy and restless, i admitted that i got the card all the time. to me, it represented imprisonment, isolation and fear - which are some of its classical interpretations. but my teacher pointed at the image on the card (we were using the rider-waite deck) and said: "oh but look, she has been left alone now. she has every reason to be afraid - someone took her somewhere and surrounded her with all of these swords and bound her and blindfolded her, but now they have left her and she is free to walk away whenever she wants, if she can just realize that she is safe."

truly, the eight of arrows is a tricky card, but it has a beautiful story. if we can get past our own beliefs, about ourselves or about the world around us, we can experience more freedom than we ever imagined possible.

many experts suggest that meditation is key to understanding the lessons held in the eight of arrows. i would suggest, too, that listening is a key component of the card. in classical versions, the figure is often shown blindfolded - here, peony has depicted the monster with wide, stressed button eyes, like a ragdoll, eyes that have been used excessively, perhaps, and cannot be trusted. listening, sinking in, can truly be of use.

EIGHT OF ARROWS, REVERSED

most frequently i see the eight of arrows reverse itself when a person is struggling against unrealistic expectations of who they are established by past behavior. it could be that the querent is in recovery and does not know how to present themselves as clean and sober; it could be they have ended a major relationship and are having trouble extricating themselves from a certain way of being known as one part of a couple; it could be that there has been a professional shift and the querent is struggling to make new boundaries according to these changes.

bottom line: don't be afraid to express your truest self. remember that old comfort quote: "those who matter don't mind, and those who mind don't matter."

NINE OF ARROWS

man, i'm sorry, but i kind of hate the nine of arrows. i mean, i love it too, because it is essential, but that doesn't change that it is super rough to turn over in a reading. there is a feeling of things getting worse, of growing calamity, of despair and desperation, of tragedy approaching. this poor little monster has so many thoughts whipping around, it is so scared.

but it is ok to be scared. there's a reason to be scared. but here's the really important thing: the actual, momentary, day-to-day details of life might not be as bad as they seem. when the nine of arrows pops up, it is an expression of all the anxiety and horror that the querent is dealing with, often in the face of tangible problems...but it is also a sign that those burdens are all being handled alone, and sometimes that they are being swallowed or denied to the point of creating significant mental strain.

don't be afraid to cry. don't be afraid to reach out. don't be afraid to process all these thoughts and feelings. they need a place to go: if they aren't processed, they can poison you.

NINE OF ARROWS, REVERSED

a lot of times when the nine of arrows turns up reversed it is a little like the three of arrows: the dam has broken, the querent has admitted challenges and struggles, and now there is room for healing. the nine of arrows reversed says that you might be feeling quite raw right now, maybe lost, maybe even hopeless, but that you are admitting it and doing something about it.

please hang in there. the nine of arrows reversed is a little like a rainbow after a storm: there is still beauty, there is still hope.

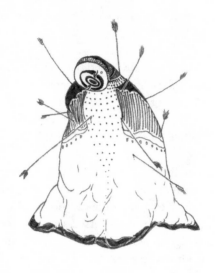

TEN OF ARROWS

ooooof. that's gotta hurt. but at the same time, there's a certain freedom in it, because the monster in the card is certainly dead. it's over. whatever has been causing you so much stress and fear and pain: IT'S OVER. done. finished.

you might be laying there burdened by the weight of this disaster, but at least you know the worst is over. because this is the transitional card between the minor and major arcana, the ten of arrows can symbolize a sort of revelation about what is truly important: all concerns of the material world transcended, we can now move on to the major spiritual lessons of our lives.

however, if we don't make the effort to truly learn from our errors, or foibles, our mistakes, we are doomed to repeat them: to start all over from the ace of wands and just go through the same patterns until we can effectively free ourselves from old karmas.

basically, the ten of arrows is about acceptance. if you can acknowledge and release, you can move on. whatever you have suffered through, it is time to leave this particular path and journey forward, and with the information you have gathered, you will be stronger than ever as you begin the next phase of life.

TEN OF ARROWS, REVERSED

let go, let go, let go. you are holding onto something that will only continue to cause you pain. the sooner you loosen your grasp, the sooner you can keep advancing forward in life. for now, look at the image: ten of arrows reversed has the corpse of the monster resting atop the arrows, on display, all that pain laid out for everyone to see. it is very obvious and a bit over-the-top, this arduous struggle. someone else may have started it, but you're continuing it by refusing to relinquish a mental attachment to what it means to you. watch out for that victim mentality, it's a doozy.

CHILD OF ARROWS

philosophy literally translates from the greek to "love of
wisdom." child of arrows is certainly a philosopher, and is
especially interested in uncovering the truth - look at those little
antennae, tuned in to the world, investigating everything.
curious, eager, attentive and perceptive, the child of arrows is a
natural communicator and seeks to understand the world
through asking questions. no stone unturned, every theory
tested, every possibility investigated. sometimes this energy,
because of the youthful inexperience of all of the children in the
courts, can move a little too quick: it can be a restless, hungry
mind that jumps from one thing to the next without fully

absorbing the lessons that are offered. it can also very easily represent a person who speaks without thinking, unwittingly spreading gossip or rumors, or hurting friends and loved ones with unsolicited advice or information.

while the mind of the child of arrows is a precious jewel, it is advisable to set that jewel carefully in something that helps direct its frenzied crystalline beam: given a mental task or problem to wrangle with, the child of arrows is a great gift. without focus, it is an undeniable hassle.

CHILD OF ARROWS, REVERSED

blah blah blah. the child of arrows reversed is all talk and no action, all bark and no bite, just a lot of empty words. take care to say what you mean, and mean what you say, and surround yourself with those who do the same.

KNIGHT OF ARROWS

the knight of arrows is undeniably impressive, quite the go-getter, and so self-assured in their ideas! with very developed communication skills and the ability to be a strong leader, the knight of arrows often represents a person or aspect of the querent who seems to have it all figured out, maybe to the point of trampling others on the way. where the child of arrows can accidentally and in all innocence say the wrong thing and remain oblivious to what they have done, the knight of arrows can sometimes be heartlessly critical and totally aware of how critical they are being.

this can be a necessary skill when one is, say, a human rights lawyer. less relevant when one is taking care of a child, or negotiating terms in a personal relationship. there is so much ferocity and cleverness in the knight of arrows, and it is just important to put these skills to proper use. be wary of berating others, or of allowing yourself to be harangued. while the knight of arrows is often correct (they have certainly thought things over, after all), they may be overly hasty or cruel for no reason other than impatience.

KNIGHT OF ARROWS, REVERSED

oh my god, stop. the knight of arrows reversed is such a shit-talker. if the knight of arrows reversed pops up, take note of the part of yourself or someone in your circle that will not stop spreading unkind information about others around. this is a troublemaking energy - there's no purpose to it at all, because it doesn't even really satisfy the restless intensity of the knight of arrows reversed. remember the expression "if you don't have anything nice to say, don't say anything at all"? yup.

QUEEN OF ARROWS

quite brilliant, the queen of arrows is in her best aspect when
she pursues situations that utilize her intellectual abilities. she is
swift-thinking, bright, clever, intelligent, keen-witted, and quite
observant. if the queens tend to represent a principle of being
loving and generous, the queen of arrows might be the "tough
love" figure, one who tells it like it is and pulls no punches. but
while she can be cold, she isn't cruel. she is very ethical, and
craves clarity in all things.

i call her "the mistress of boundaries." she is good at figuring
things out. whether good at sticking to the boundaries she

knows she ought to have is another story entirely, and likely up to the querent to decide.

in peony's depiction, notice how the queen of arrows sits before a flowering shrub that has buried within it several arrows. do they belong to the queen? or were they fired at her? the answer is probably both: while they may have been used against her at one point, the queen of arrows has taken them for her own. you see, the queen of swords learns from her own experiences, and transforms any attack against her to expertise. she can use the injuries in her past to make educated decisions about her future. she is always changing, shifting, as the situation demands. but there is a downside to this, which is that without consulting the heart or the spiritual instincts, the queen of arrows can make defensive choices almost automatically, and can keep herself withdrawn and isolated due to past hurts and conflicts. if she has a downfall, it is her ability to project a cool and aloof demeanor above her true feelings, almost to the point where she may come to believe in her own façade.

QUEEN OF ARROWS, REVERSED

the queen of arrows reversed is so certain she is right about something that she lashes out. she rejects closeness, compassion, the complications of friendship, because she is unforgiving in her expectations for ethical perfection. she is unwilling to wade into the nuances of relationship, choosing instead to sit in a tower of moral superiority and pack her heart with ice.

if the queen of arrows reversed turns up for you, lighten up on the situation. stop overthinking it. in fact, try not thinking at all for a bit. give yourself a break. things will probably be fine.

KING OF ARROWS

here is the very embodiment of aquarius, who can be argued to be perhaps the truest humanitarian of the zodiac. strangely, aquarius so loves the world by being oddly removed from it at times: way up high in the starry ether, studying humanity as algorithms, rhythms, patterns, rather than as individuals or specific circumstances. the king of arrows is so good at this distant adoration. surrounding him are butterflies, traditionally associated with the arrows (or swords) as a symbol of the active mind - the butterflies flit from one thought to the next as easily as anything, alighting briefly on one mental flower before moving effortlessly onto the next. the king of arrows can cycle through seemingly disparate thoughts with ease and grace, moving from a practical matter to an emotional crisis to a philosophical query more quickly than maybe anyone else.

because of this, he has profound clarity as his ally. logic and intellect serve him well and insulate him from failure. there is a beautiful sharpness to his keen mind - a knife well-honed. he is fair and just, even-tempered and influential. he is an expert, an authority.

if the king of arrows turns up in your reading, look for a part of yourself or a person you know who is utilizing their powers of discernment. trust that you have the resources you need to make an accurate decision.

KING OF ARROWS, REVERSED

the king of arrows reversed can be a tyrant, using information that he has to control circumstances. this could be through deception, omission, or through brutal and unnecessary honesty. being so detached from emotions can make a person vicious and unsympathetic. the best thing to do here is disengage, if possible. whether this card represents your actions or someone else's, time apart is indicated to avoid ongoing emotional abuse.

ACKNOWLEDGEMENTS

as with, perhaps, all things in life, this project would not have been possible without the gracious support of many. crowd-funding has opened a new portal in the world that allows for creative works to receive generosity from friends and strangers alike.

we extend our humblest gratitude to all of our kickstarter supporters, but especially:

claire r., rosie lee, j chris schmidt, gia mancini-mccormick, cynthia gonsalves, rebecca redwood and clayton phillips, elayne riven, mixel pixel, turk pipkin, lisa oppel, jared & constance watkins, chris mcdowall, bradley everett cathcart, buster benson, christy pipkin, blue bird johnson, mj foley, moboid, harry and elizabeth anderson, fodejo, melissa cynova, l toop, piot boris, elizabeth brek lloyd, k. macdonald, hunter ellinger & mary parker, annie nelson, william riot, martha bodell, judith nast, linda and howard mccollum, kathleen painter, jamie, & one anonymous supporter

the businesses who supported us by buying advance bulk orders are:

crystal works, blackmail boutique & charm school vintage

olivia also wishes to thank:

my many mentors and clients over the years who have assisted me in a deeper understanding of the sacred tradition of the tarot, and especially my apprentices, who have always taught me as much as i have taught them.

ABOUT THE AUTHORS

peony coin archer - illustrator

peony coin archer is a longtime illustrator of esoterica, with two published tarot decks, as well as several gem and mineral decks and a coloring book. she lives in pittsburgh, pennsylvania with a cat and many plants and stones.

olivia ephraim pepper - writer

olivia ephraim pepper is a wandering mystic, gnostic chaplain, writer and artist who wanders the face of the earth in search of knowledge. olivia has cooperated with peony on several projects and has read tarot cards since the age of 6.